CODE OF SILENCE

CODE OF SILENCE

HOW ONE HONEST POLICE OFFICER TOOK ON AUSTRALIA'S MOST CORRUPT POLICE FORCE

COLIN DILLON
WITH TOM GILLING

ALLEN&UNWIN
SYDNEY · MELBOURNE · AUCKLAND · LONDON

First published in 2016
This edition published in 2017

Copyright © Colin Dillon and Tom Gilling 2016

All rights reserved. No part of this book may be reproduced or transmitted in any form or by any means, electronic or mechanical, including photocopying, recording or by any information storage and retrieval system, without prior permission in writing from the publisher. The Australian *Copyright Act 1968* (the Act) allows a maximum of one chapter or 10 per cent of this book, whichever is the greater, to be photocopied by any educational institution for its educational purposes provided that the educational institution (or body that administers it) has given a remuneration notice to the Copyright Agency (Australia) under the Act.

Allen & Unwin
83 Alexander Street
Crows Nest NSW 2065
Australia
Phone: (61 2) 8425 0100
Email: info@allenandunwin.com
Web: www.allenandunwin.com

Cataloguing-in-Publication details are available
from the National Library of Australia
www.trove.nla.gov.au

ISBN 978 1 76029 702 2

Set in Sabon by Midland Typesetters, Australia

Printed and bound in Australia by Griffin Press

10 9 8 7 6 5 4 3

The paper in this book is FSC® certified. FSC® promotes environmentally responsible, socially beneficial and economically viable management of the world's forests.

Contents

About this book		vii
1	Honest police, please come forward	1
2	'I've wanted to be a policeman ever since I was a boy'	9
3	Doing things differently	17
4	Licensing Branch	25
5	SP bookies . . . a protected species	41
6	A bottle of whisky	55
7	The code	67
8	The black cat	79
9	Lifting the lid	85
10	Fronting the Fitzgerald Inquiry	95
11	Doing things as they should be done	109
12	An undercover officer's cover is blown	121
13	Hitting a brick wall	131
14	The most unwanted job in the police force	141
15	An unbridgeable rift	157
16	Whistleblowers	169
17	Flying the flag for NAIDOC Week	173
18	Would things ever change?	191
19	The rise and rise of Detective Tony Murphy	211
20	'You used to be an inspector in the police force, didn't you?'	219
Epilogue		231

About this book

Colin Dillon joined the Queensland Police in 1965, two years before the nationwide referendum that was supposed to mark the end of official discrimination and guarantee full and equal citizenship for Aboriginal Australians. During the four decades he served as a police officer he was promoted to become Australia's first Indigenous police inspector.

Dillon was the first serving officer to voluntarily give concrete evidence of police corruption to the Fitzgerald Commission of Inquiry in 1987. His evidence helped send a number of corrupt police and politicians, including the commissioner of police, to prison.

This book tells the story of an honest man's nearly 40-year career in a police force that was rotten to the core. It reveals the extraordinary range of criminal activities—drugs, gaming, SP bookmaking, brothels, vehicle theft—that were allowed to operate with impunity in return for bribes. It describes attempts by corrupt colleagues to bribe and intimidate Dillon into keeping his mouth shut. Dillon remained in the police force for many years after the Fitzgerald Inquiry. During that time he and his family paid a high price for his decision to break the code of silence. While a number of officers who admitted their corruption were given witness protection, Dillon was left to protect himself and his family at a time when his life was under constant threat.

Code of Silence was written in the hope of inspiring others to speak out when they know things are not right. By shining a light on corruption they will not only expose wrongdoers but empower those who are behaving honestly.

Wherever there is power and money, there is always the risk of corruption. But everyone has a choice: to become involved or to take a stand against it.

QUEENSLAND POLICE SERVICE

CERTIFICATE OF SERVICE

COLIN WILLIAM MAXWELL DILLON

served as a member of the Queensland Police Service from 31 March 1965 to 6 April 2001. After 36 years loyal and dedicated service to the community of Queensland, and having attained the rank of Inspector he retired from the Service.

Awards Granted:		
	Queensland Police Service Medal and 30 year Clasp	1999
	Australian Police Medal	1992
	Police Long Service and and Good Conduct Medal	1987
	Commendation	1979
	Commendation	1966

Served as Probationary: 11 January 1965 to 30 March 1965

COMMISSIONER

The oath of office sworn by each Queensland police constable, under the *Police Service Administration Act 1990*, before they may take up their duties:

> I ... swear by Almighty God that I will well and truly serve our Sovereign Lady Queen Elizabeth the Second and Her Heirs and Successors according to law in the office of constable or in such other capacity as I may be hereafter appointed, promoted or reduced, without favour or affection, malice or ill will, from this date and until I am legally discharged; that I will cause Her Majesty's peace to be kept and preserved; that I will prevent to the best of my power all offences against the same, and that while I shall continue to be a member of the Queensland Police Service I will to the best of my skill and knowledge discharge all the duties legally imposed upon me faithfully and according to law. So help me God.

ONE

Honest police, please come forward

I contacted the Fitzgerald Commission of Inquiry by telephone on Wednesday, 9 September 1987, the day after being discharged from Prince Charles Hospital, Brisbane where I had undergone heart surgery. After stating my name, address, rank and where I was stationed, I said that I wanted to come in to talk about my time at the Licensing Branch. The person who answered said that I would be contacted in due course but that it was not possible to give me a date. It seemed to me that he didn't care whether I came in or not. The lukewarm response was a bitter disappointment after all the agonising that had gone into my decision to make the call. I consoled myself with the thought that other honest cops would soon be coming forward to tell the commission what they knew about corruption in the Queensland Police. Little did I know that most of the honest cops would remain silent.

Detective Senior Sergeant Harry Burgess, who was up to his neck in corruption, had already confessed to taking bribes. As a result of Burgess's admissions, on 31 August 1987 Commissioner Fitzgerald had declared that 'the issue is no more whether there was any corruption as how much and by whom'. He went on to say:

> This inquiry is going to succeed with or without the information provided by honest policemen. Without that information it may be harder and it may take longer but the result will be the same ... We are quite aware of the desperate campaign which is being waged within the force to seek to maintain the closed ranks which provide a shelter for any culprits.

I did not need Fitzgerald or anyone else to tell me what it would mean to break ranks. I hadn't slept properly for weeks. My stress levels were through the roof. I had recently suffered a near-fatal heart attack and was still recuperating from follow-up heart surgery. I had been inside enough courtrooms to know that once I was in the witness box I would be subject to relentless cross-examination by lawyers being paid to destroy my credibility. I knew that the people I was accusing of corruption would do everything they could to intimidate me. When the moment of truth came, would I stand strong or would I buckle? I really didn't know.

At about 8 p.m. on Sunday, 13 September 1987 I was surprised to hear a knock at my front door. I answered and was greeted by Ralph Devlin, junior counsel assisting the Fitzgerald Inquiry. He hadn't bothered to telephone me beforehand to let me know he was coming. We went upstairs to my study where Devlin told me that he had come to take a statement from me about my service at the Licensing Branch. He had brought an A4-sized writing pad on which he scribbled notes. I told him that it would be far better for me to be interviewed at the commission's offices where I could give my statement and have it typed up in one go, but Devlin explained that the commission was short-staffed and that the only way they could keep on top of their work was by interviewing witnesses at weekends.

I remember saying to him that I hoped other police were coming forward to give supporting evidence of corruption, because without their corroboration it would be impossible to flush out the system.

Devlin's response was, 'Don't worry, Col. You've got a lot of mates following you.'

Talking to Ralph Devlin at home in my study was one thing, but the thought of giving evidence in public was giving me the terrors. I told Devlin I was worried about my health. The pressure was killing me. I said I needed a couple of weeks to pull myself together before giving evidence and Devlin gave me the impression that the commissioner was prepared to wait. Two days later I received a call from a lawyer called Pat Nolan, representing the Queensland Police Union of Employees. He said, 'Col, I have been contacted by the senior staff at the inquiry and they have advised me that they need you to appear and give evidence tomorrow.'

I was shocked. 'Pat, it's too soon,' I said. 'I'm buggered. I don't think I can do it.'

Pat replied, 'I don't know whether or not you are aware that Commissioner Fitzgerald made a public call for honest police to come forward as well as members of the public and he didn't get a single response. They need you to take the stand tomorrow or the inquiry is in real danger of shutting down. I can let Fitzgerald's people know about your health so hopefully they can get you through your evidence quickly.'

I felt as if I had been backed into a corner but it was too late to do anything about it. 'OK, Pat,' I said. 'I'll be there.'

I had thought that I could have a couple of weeks to get my health sorted out before taking the stand, but the truth was the inquiry needed my evidence now. Burgess had confessed in return for an indemnity against prosecution, but Blind Freddie could see that he wasn't telling everything he knew. There had been evidence from a parlour madam and some illegal casino operators, but not all of it could be trusted. What the commission needed was concrete evidence of corruption from witnesses with nothing to hide; that was why Mr Fitzgerald had pleaded for honest police to come forward. Right now the only one they had was me. The night before I testified to the Fitzgerald Inquiry was one of the worst of my life. I was a nervous wreck. I hadn't yet told my wife, Linda, that I was going to give evidence, although she had been following the progress of the inquiry in the newspapers and knew that its main focus would be on the Licensing Branch, where I had been working until a few months earlier. Nor had I mentioned it to my children, Anthony and Sandra, both of whom were still at school: Anthony in his second year of high school and Sandra in her final year at primary. They were both old enough to know and they had every right to know. Of course neither I nor anyone else had any inkling of how big this was going to be, but I was sure that once the inquiry started, the media were going to be all over it. It would be an ordeal for the kids and I knew I owed it to them to warn them, but right now I was in no state to do it.

After the children went to bed I finally summoned up the courage to tell Linda. Throughout my career I had made a point of not bringing my job home. Other blokes might have been happy discussing police work around the dinner table but I never could. When I explained that I would be giving evidence the next day, she stared at me in silence, as if she was trying to work out what thoughts were going through my head. Then she said, 'Whatever you do, Col, make sure you don't dob on anybody. You know what will happen if you do. You'll end up having to leave the force—what would we do then? It's the only job you know.'

'Never dob on your mates' was a motto that could apply to people in any walk of life. But in the police it was more than just a motto: it was an unbreakable law. Anybody who broke that law knew they would never be forgiven.

I prayed for a long time that night, asking God for the inner strength I would need to give my evidence and face up to the hostile cross-examination that was certain to follow.

It was dawn before I knew it. As soon as Linda got up, I suggested that she take the kids and spend a few days with her mother and sister, who had rented a unit on the north coast for a week. The calmness she had showed the night before had vanished. She asked me why I had to give evidence at all. She wanted to know what I was planning to say. I tried to reassure her that it wasn't just me—everyone who had worked at the Licensing Branch would be called before the inquiry and questioned about corruption.

As for what I was planning to say, I told her that all I would be doing was stating my name, rank and registered number and telling them how long I had served at the Licensing Branch. There was nothing else I could tell them, I said, because I didn't know any more. It wasn't true, but I felt that the only way I could stand up and testify about the corruption I had witnessed was if I reassured my wife that she had nothing to fear. Linda seemed relieved and agreed to join her mother and sister on the north coast. She promised to phone me that night.

I travelled to work that morning the same way I always did—in full uniform, crammed shoulder to shoulder with other commuters on the train to Roma Street Station in the heart of Brisbane. I couldn't help noticing the huge headlines on the front page of the *Courier Mail* about the start of the Fitzgerald Inquiry. Maybe I was imagining it but I could feel strangers looking up from their papers and staring at me, wondering whether I was one of the corrupt police they had been reading about.

From Roma Street Station it was a 100-metre walk to my office at Police Headquarters in Makerston Street. It wasn't too long before I received a telephone call from Pat Nolan asking me to come to his office to meet Leon Taeffe, the barrister who would be appearing for the police unions. Pat and Leon would then accompany me to the Commission of Inquiry's office in Ann Street near North Quay.

As soon as I arrived, Leon told me that he had made the commissioner, Tony Fitzgerald, and his team aware of my medical condition. I had seen Leon perform many times over the years in a variety of courts. He was a top-drawer defence barrister and I felt he was being straight with me. He said, 'Col, I will be at the bar table the whole time. If you feel crook or you need a spell, just give me a nod and I'll see that you are given a break.'

At the same time Leon reminded me that Fitzgerald was relying on my evidence to keep the inquiry moving. His words only added to the pressure I was already under.

After we arrived at Ann Street, Pat and Leon left me in the company of two minders from the commission's staff, who took me to a small windowless room on the ground floor. The room felt stuffy and claustrophobic but when I asked if we could go somewhere else, they told me that this was the only room available. They said they didn't want to run the risk of my being seen by any of the police who had been seconded to the inquiry. That didn't exactly fill me with confidence.

Both of them were clutching hand-held radios that enabled them to monitor what was going on inside the courtroom. The longer we stayed cooped up in that airless room, the worse I felt. At one point I thought I was going to be sick. I asked to go to the toilet but at that moment one of the minders started shepherding me towards the door. 'Quick,' he said. 'We have to move. You're on next.'

HONEST POLICE, PLEASE COME FORWARD

We hurried down a narrow corridor and out onto Ann Street, then crossed the road and climbed a flight of stairs that led to the spacious courtyard of the Supreme and District Courts complex. TV and radio crews were jostling outside. The media's appetite for 'mystery witnesses' had already been whetted by a parlour madam who came to the hearings disguised in a huge blonde wig and sunglasses and gave evidence from behind a wooden screen. Since Fitzgerald had made his offer of indemnity there had been a steady trickle of rumours about unnamed police coming forward. When they saw me, the reporters in the courtyard put two and two together and decided I must be the inquiry's new 'secret' witness. They rushed towards me, but before they could ask any questions my two minders bundled me indoors, where I was quickly scanned and my personal details entered in the attendance book. We took a lift to the second floor and waited in a small room just across the corridor from court number 27, where the inquiry was under way.

I was still praying, as I had been ever since the night before. I knew the moment of truth was about to arrive.

After a while one of the minders said, 'You're on!'

I jumped out of my chair and started moving towards the door, only for him to pull me back with the words, 'Hang on, it's a false alarm.'

By now my nerves were pretty much shredded. I wasn't even sure I'd be able to make it through the door to the courtroom. 'If you bastards call a false alarm once more,' I growled, 'I'm out of here.'

'Sorry, mate,' one of them said. 'We know it must be tough for you.'

I snapped back, 'You wouldn't have a bloody clue what it's like for me, so don't give me that bullshit.'

Another ten minutes or so went by before I heard my name called out over the speakers in the corridor. It was called three times, which is the normal practice. This time it was no false alarm.

I stood up and felt a surge of power run through my body. I no longer felt sick or nervous. Feeling that God had answered my prayers, I strode confidently into the courtroom.

Every seat in the main body of the court was taken. There must have been journalists from every newspaper in Australia. Members of the public were packed like sardines into the upper gallery. In their eagerness to catch every word that was said, some people in the front row were leaning so far over the gallery rail that I thought they might topple out.

I entered the witness box and took the Bible in my right hand while the clerk of the court administered the oath. Then I placed my cap on the bench beside me. After glancing up at the spectators in the gallery, I turned to face the phalanx of lawyers: Queen's Counsel, senior counsel, instructing solicitors, and numerous juniors and clerks. In all my years as a police officer I had never seen so many lawyers gathered at the same time in a single courtroom, and most were itching for the chance to tear me to shreds. I felt like Daniel in the lions' den.

Commissioner Fitzgerald looked at me and I nodded to indicate that I was ready to begin. I took a deep breath. Once I started telling the inquiry about what I knew, there would be no going back. How would I get through it? Would it be the end of my policing career? What would be the effect on my family?

I was about to find out.

TWO

'I've wanted to be a policeman ever since I was a boy'

Both my parents are descendants of the Kombumerri people of the Yugambeh nation, whose traditional grounds stretch from the northern bank of the Tweed River on the Queensland–New South Wales border to the banks of the Logan River at Beenleigh, and from the ocean foreshores to the edge of the Great Dividing Range. My ancestors' country takes in all of what is known today as Queensland's Gold Coast and its environs.

My people lived mainly along the banks of the Nerang River in the heart of Kombumerri country. It was in this fertile country that, before colonisation, they hunted and gathered fish and crustaceans, supplemented by the seasonal wild fruits, nuts and berries that were abundant in the lush rainforest of the Gold Coast Hinterland.

My father and mother lived in Southport on the banks of the beautiful Nerang River before moving to the seaside township of Caloundra some 90 kilometres north-east of

Brisbane. I was born on 10 May 1944, at the end of World War II, in the small rural town of Nambour, the second of eleven children.

My siblings, in order of age, were my brother Keith (deceased); sister Theresa (Tess); brother Michael (deceased); sister Marie; sister Patsy; brother Luke; brother Earl; sister Eve; sister Joanne (deceased) and my youngest sister, Hilma.

When the war began my father was an apprentice tailor—an industry designated as an essential service for its role in making uniforms for Australia's armed forces. While working as a tailor he received a white feather—a hangover from World War I, when women were urged to send white feathers to men out of uniform in order to shame them into volunteering. Dad was devastated; he was pretty sure he knew who had sent it—an auntie by marriage whom he had never liked. Dad was no coward. He was eager to serve his country and longed to be with his cousins who were already serving, some in Papua New Guinea and a couple in the Middle East. (Two of his cousins died in the war, one killed in action by the Japanese in New Guinea and another as a prisoner of war in Sandakan.)

As soon as he was able, Dad joined the Australian Army Provost Corps (the military police) as a corporal. It was a tense time in Australia as the Japanese were pushing south and there seemed to be a real risk of invasion. The high rate of desertion among Australian troops made Dad's job as an MP both demanding and dangerous. It was a strict rule for MPs to work in pairs as deserters would often do anything to evade arrest, but it didn't always happen. Acting on a tip-off, Dad went alone one day to an address in Toowoomba.

While the woman who lived there loudly denied that she was harbouring a deserter, she motioned to a backyard shed and mouthed the words, *'He's in there.'* As my father approached the door of the shed, the deserter came out swinging an axe, which forced my father to draw his pistol.

'I'VE WANTED TO BE A POLICEMAN EVER SINCE I WAS A BOY'

My father was anxious to avoid shooting, so he kept his distance and tried to persuade the man to surrender. The man put down his axe but produced the largest roll of twenty-pound notes my father had ever seen—offering it all to him in exchange for letting him go.

In telling that story, my father made sure I understood the implications of a bribe. He went to great lengths to explain what temptation and greed did to people and how a bribe worked like a steel trap—once you accepted a bribe there was no way out. Dad knew of my ambition to one day join the police force and I believe his stories were a deliberate attempt to pass on important lessons and values that would be helpful to me in my own career.

Later in the war my father fought against the Japanese in Bougainville and the Solomon Islands. One day in dense jungle he had become separated from his mates and found himself standing on the banks of a deep and fast-flowing stream. Looking up, he caught sight of an armed Japanese soldier staring at him across the stream. He had seconds to decide what to do but Dad's instinct was to preserve life wherever possible. He also realised that there could be more enemy nearby, who would come running if they heard a shot. Aiming his rifle at the Japanese soldier, he motioned for to him to put his weapon on the ground and to cross the stream. The Japanese soldier followed my father's instructions and allowed himself to be taken prisoner.

When questioned later, the soldier insisted that he had become lost in the jungle after being separated from his unit—the same as my father. The Australians were sceptical but he was probably telling the truth because there was no contact with the enemy after he was captured.

My youngest brother, Earl, told me the fate of the Japanese soldier 60 years after the war ended. The soldier managed to track down my father and write him a letter thanking him for sparing his life. In the letter he confessed that he had never wanted to go to war as, like Dad, he could not see the point in killing. Apparently he returned to his profession as a school teacher after the war.

While fighting in the Solomon Islands my father contracted malaria, like many of his mates, and went on to suffer recurrent bouts throughout his life. One attack, before I started primary school, made him shake violently despite my auntie's attempts to break the fever by piling blankets over him. I remember worrying that he was going to die.

Along with thousands of families during the final years of World War II, we were poor. The war caused many hardships and there was a scarcity of any meaningful employment. Even after the war ended coupons were used for a short time as a means of rationing essential food and other necessary items.

After returning from the war, my father started up a milk run. There wasn't much money in it and many of his customers could not afford to pay for their milk. Dad soon realised that the business wasn't viable and that he would have to look for something else.

Work of any kind remained hard to find. Caloundra in those days was just a little seaside town, off the beaten track. Its small businesses were heavily reliant on holidaymakers visiting over Easter and Christmas. Eventually my father got a job in a sawmill at Beerwah, where he worked long hours on the saw bench dressing timber for very meagre wages. He considered himself lucky to have found any work at all.

After a couple of years at the sawmill he was taken on as a barman at the old Hotel Caloundra at Shelly Beach, which back then was the only hotel in Caloundra. It was owned by the Stewart family, who had been successful hoteliers in Melbourne before coming to Caloundra. My father worked for Paddy Stewart, who eventually took over the family business. He and Paddy remained great friends for the rest of their lives.

'I'VE WANTED TO BE A POLICEMAN EVER SINCE I WAS A BOY'

I did most of my primary schooling at the Caloundra State School except for six months at the Star of the Sea Convent at Southport.

I have fond memories of my school years at Caloundra. One of the teachers I admired most was Alan Marsh, who taught me in grade eight. Mr Marsh was a returned soldier who had seen action and been decorated in World War II. The first congratulatory letter I received after giving evidence at the Fitzgerald Inquiry was from Alan. I immediately drove out to see him at the veterans' retirement home in Moggil where he was living. By then he was in poor health. I remembered him with the looks and physical features of John Wayne and was shocked to see him looking so frail. It was an emotional meeting for both of us.

As a young boy most of my leisure time was spent with my mates kicking a football around the local sports field or swimming down at Bulcock Beach on the Bribie Island passage. Bulcock Beach had pristine waters that were flushed daily by the tides. Because of its calm waters, Bulcock Beach was where most of us learnt to swim. From there we graduated to Kings Beach, where we bodysurfed on huge waves while learning how to navigate the treacherous rips. Kings Beach was also popular with the girls, which was an added attraction for us.

At about fifteen I left school and started looking for work. I had a good mate named Doug Shepherd who was apprenticed to his father who was a builder. Doug had almost finished his apprenticeship and he told me that his father would soon be looking for someone to replace him. Ever since I was a young boy I had wanted to join the police force, but I knew it would be at least four years until I was eligible, so in the meantime I decided to take up Doug's suggestion and start learning the building trade.

I enjoyed working with Doug and his brother Tom but it didn't take me long to realise that building wasn't for me. I had no trouble with menial jobs like mixing concrete and painting house stumps with creosote and I wasn't too bad at laying and nail punching timber floors (except for the bruised fingers). Then one morning Doug told me I was going to help put up some roof trusses. Doug, Tom and their father could run and skip across the trusses with the grace of a gazelle, while I crawled like a spider, terrified of missing my footing and falling. That was when I knew I wasn't cut out to be a builder. Needless to say, I gave my notice before my probationary period was up.

In his spare time Doug was an honorary ambulance bearer with the Caloundra branch of the Queensland Ambulance Transport Brigade (QATB). Doug didn't hold my roofing efforts against me and asked me one day if I would be interested in coming along. I jumped at the chance. I sat for and passed all of my first aid examinations with high distinctions. As a fully qualified first aid giver I could have applied for a full-time position, but my heart was still set on becoming a member of the Queensland Police Force. But my time with the QATB was far from wasted, and the experience and skills I gained proved invaluable when I found myself dealing with the road accidents, fights and attempted suicides that are the lot of every uniformed police officer.

Now that my building career was over, I needed another job. The father of one of my old schoolmates was the local postmaster. He heard that I was looking for work and offered to put in a word for me with the postmaster at the Ipswich Post Office, where there were a couple of casual vacancies. Ipswich, I thought—where the bloody hell is that? I was almost eighteen and apart from holidays at my grandfather's place at Southport when I was a young boy and those six months at the Star of the Sea Convent, I had never been away from Caloundra. It was where all my friends lived and where I played football at the weekends. But I knew I couldn't just

'I'VE WANTED TO BE A POLICEMAN EVER SINCE I WAS A BOY'

sit on my backside so I thanked him and said if there was a job at Ipswich, I'd be happy to take it.

The problem was I didn't own a car and getting from Caloundra to Ipswich involved catching two trains. I'd be spending half the day travelling. The only solution was for me to move to Ipswich. I had no idea how to go about finding a place to stay. I happened to mention to my local priest that I would soon be moving to Ipswich to work as a postman. He knew the priest in Ipswich, who was able to sort out some accommodation for me at a boarding house run by a Catholic family.

The boarding house was old but well looked after, a Queenslander with open verandas at the front and along one side. I shared a room with a bloke who had arrived in Australia quite recently from one of the eastern bloc countries in Europe. He was much older than me and spoke with a very heavy accent. The two of us got on all right but he had a mate, a fellow countryman, who was always drunk and who took a set against me from the start. He was always making snide comments and trying to goad me into reacting. I wasn't scared of him because I was in good physical condition, but my father warned me not to get into a fight with him. He told me he knew about blokes like that; they would shirk an honest fight but would pull a weapon on you when your back was turned. I was glad of his advice, although it meant I didn't get much sleep because I used to lie there with one eye open, just in case.

Every day on my way to the post office I had to walk past the Ipswich Police Headquarters. One afternoon an elderly sergeant was standing outside the station. As I walked past he said, 'Hello. What's your name?'

At that time I was quite shy and lacking in self-confidence. I told him my name and in the next breath he said, 'You're a fine stamp of a young fellow. Have you ever thought of joining the police force?'

I couldn't believe my ears. 'Yes,' I told him excitedly. 'I've wanted to be a policeman ever since I was a boy.'

He smiled and said, 'Come up to my office, lad. I'll get you an application form and we'll fill it out.'

Once I had signed on the dotted line, he gave me a spelling test, after which he told me to buy a spelling book, which I did.

One of the characters I had got to know on my mail run was a police constable who directed traffic and helped children at a school crossing. A week or so after my interview at the police station, he said to me, 'I need to tell you something and I hope you won't be too offended. There is a sergeant at my station who has heard about you from the senior sergeant who interviewed you last week. When he found out that you wanted to join the police force, he told the senior sergeant that if you were posted to the same station, he would refuse to walk down the same side of the street as you.' He told me the sergeant was a nasty piece of work and gave me his name in case our paths should ever cross.

I was stunned. The constable must have realised how hard I had taken it because he said, 'Try not to let it worry you because the senior sergeant is happy that you have signed up and so am I and so are plenty of others at the station.'

I appreciated his support but it took me a long time to get over what he had told me.

THREE

Doing things differently

I sometimes wonder how my career in the police force would have turned out if I had never joined the Licensing Branch. When I appeared before the Fitzgerald Inquiry I had been a serving policeman for more than twenty years, but the only part of my career that seemed to matter was the two years I had spent as a plain clothes sergeant in the Licensing Branch.

The branch had had a shady reputation almost from its inception in the early 1950s. Even within the Queensland Police, it was widely considered to be a cesspit of corruption. This was not a deterrent for me as my father had instilled in me a strong sense of right and wrong. I was 41 years old and had reached a stage in my life and career where I felt confident, sure and capable. If there were corrupt elements in the Licensing Branch, as many suspected, I knew that I would not be sucked in.

Staffed by detectives and by plain clothes officers who aspired to become detectives, the Licensing Branch was responsible for enforcing the laws relating to prostitution, illegal gaming and starting price (SP) betting. It had begun life as the Vice Squad until the conservative government of the day renamed it the Licensing Branch—a title that was less accurate but more palatable to Queensland citizens.

My career in the police had taken me from Innisfail in far north Queensland to Newmarket and Toowong in suburban Brisbane, with stints at the Juvenile Delinquency Squad and the Police Communications Centre. My last posting before the Licensing Branch was at the Brisbane Regional Task Force, dealing mostly with street offences. I had enjoyed my time there but I wanted to broaden my experience. Working in the Licensing Branch would show me a different side of policing.

On the Saturday before I was officially transferred to the Licensing Branch, I went to introduce myself to my new colleagues. I was met by Detective Senior Sergeant Allen Bulger, the second-in-charge. I had seen Bulger before but did not know him, nor did he know me. Bulger was a big man, an overweight smoker with a florid complexion. I guessed he was a heavy drinker. (My assessment proved to be close to the mark.) He was also passionate about horse-racing and—I soon found out—a reckless punter.

Bulger gave me a friendly welcome. We chatted for a while and he apologised that the officer-in-charge, Detective Inspector Graeme Parker, was not available. He added that I would be interviewed by Parker when I formally joined the branch. What he didn't know was that Graeme Parker and I had served together at Innisfail some eighteen years earlier. I was then a young uniform constable and Parker was a detective senior constable in the Criminal Investigation Branch (CIB).

I knew for certain that Parker had been corrupt while he was at Innisfail and it was disconcerting to find that he was now in charge of the Licensing Branch.

DOING THINGS DIFFERENTLY

As I chatted with Bulger I wondered whether he knew about Frank's Gaming House (or Gambling Den, as most of the locals called it). Innisfail's Gambling Den operated as a social club where men of all ethnic backgrounds came to relax and socialise. When I was working in that town I had known that Frank was paying Parker as well as two other members of the local CIB and a uniformed senior sergeant in return for being allowed to continue his lucrative backroom business of illegal gaming.

As young uniformed constables, we had all been lectured by the station senior sergeant at Innisfail that under no circumstances were we to enter any of the several ethnic clubs within the Innisfail district. He didn't give us any reason why these clubs were 'no go' areas for young uniformed police other than to say it was strictly the domain and responsibility of CIB personnel to check these premises if and when required.

I was well aware of the senior sergeant's instructions as I stood outside one of these 'clubs' in the main street of Innisfail with Constable Jock Carlyle one night in 1966. It was after midnight and there was plenty of activity inside. Curious to know what was going on, we debated whether to sneak around the back and have a look. Jock wasn't keen, but I said that as police officers we had every right to check the premises to see that no offences were being committed. Eventually, Jock agreed. We pushed our way through shoulder-high guinea grass in a vacant block next to the club and hoisted ourselves up on two concrete posts that enabled us to see without being seen.

Through the old galvanised window we saw a large oblong table covered in paper money of all denominations. The patrons were all male and obviously from different ethnic backgrounds. It confirmed what most of us young constables already suspected: that the 'clubs' were in fact gambling dens.

We clambered down off the concrete posts and Jock asked gingerly, 'What do we do now?'

I knew that he was hoping I would say, 'Let's get out of here.' I looked him in the eye and said, 'Jock, we've got to go in.'

We thumped on the solid timber door. The door opened and we were cheerfully greeted by a man we knew as a respectable local businessman. His name was Frank. In the smoke-filled room Jock and I recognised some businessmen and a few local cane farmers, all of whom seemed completely relaxed about our unexpected visit.

I told Frank that we were there in an official, not a social capacity. I pointed out that he and all those present were in breach of the law and that Jock and I intended to take appropriate action. Frank looked at me with a huge grin—he thought I was joking.

Jock said, 'What are we going to do? We can't arrest everyone here, not the two of us.'

'We're not going to arrest everyone,' I said. 'We'll just take their names and addresses. We can take action by way of complaint and summons at a later date.'

As we started to take the names and addresses of the gamblers, Frank's grin disappeared. He motioned with his hand towards the piles of money on the table. 'Col,' he said. 'What are you after? You and Jock can take what you want.'

'Stop there, Frank,' I said. 'That's not what we're about. You fellows are breaking the law and we're here to put a stop to it.'

A bewildered look came over his face. He said, 'Col, don't you know we have permission to run these games? We've always had permission to run them.'

If Jock was worried before, he was twice as worried now.

I told Frank, 'Neither of us is aware of the person you say is giving you permission to gamble in these premises.

Are you prepared to tell me who you are paying for permission to run the games here?'

Without a moment's hesitation, Frank replied, 'The CIB and your boss.'

I asked for their names. Frank said, 'Your boss, Senior Sergeant Harry; Graeme Parker; Jimmy Wilson; and their boss, Jack.'

Jock looked at me and I looked back at him. Neither of us said a word but I knew we were both thinking the same thing: 'What the hell have we got ourselves into?'

We continued to write down names and addresses, ignoring pleas from several of the gamblers for us not to use their real names or occupations.

After leaving the club, Jock and I had a serious conversation about whether or not to instigate prosecutions against the gamblers whose details we had taken. We were very junior and inexperienced constables, still well within the twelve-month training and probationary period, during which we could be discharged from the police force with no reason given and without any right of redress or avenue for appeal. Young as we were, we had enough nous to know that we had bitten off more than we could chew and that going ahead with the prosecutions could end our careers before they had begun.

Reluctantly, we made up our minds to forget what we had seen and prayed that neither Frank nor any of his friends would report back to the station senior sergeant, or to Parker and his two CIB colleagues, about our unauthorised visit. For several weeks afterwards both Jock and I lived in fear of being summoned to the senior sergeant's office and asked to explain ourselves.

As well as Frank's club there were at least five more ethnic clubs in the Innisfail district where people could happily go to drink and gamble. None of them could have operated without police protection.

Little did I know that what I had learnt about Parker in Innisfail would save my skin when we met again eighteen years later in the Licensing Branch.

* * *

As I stood talking to Allen Bulger, my mind went back to that night in Innisfail. Was it possible that Frank had told Parker that I knew he and others in the Innisfail CIB were on the take? If he had, surely Parker would have done his best to get rid of me. At the very least he would have tried to block my transfer to the Licensing Branch.

The commissioner of police, Terry (later Sir Terence) Lewis, made a point of personally ringing officers to confirm promotions and transfers. I remembered the matey phone call from Lewis that confirmed my transfer from the regional task force: 'Hi, old fellow, just phoning to congratulate you and let you know that I have approved your transfer to the Licensing Branch. You applied for it so you obviously want to go there.'

I had thanked Lewis for his confidence in me and for giving me the opportunity to widen my experience in the force. I told him I would give the new job my best shot.

Lewis replied, 'I've got no doubts about that. You have done excellent work to date, particularly at Toowong and in the task force. Take care and all the best, old fellow. I'll be following your career with interest.'

This was the second transfer the commissioner had approved for me. I appreciated his call and admired his informality— *How are you going, old fellow?*—and the concern he had always shown for the welfare of the officers he commanded. But it wasn't long before I started wondering just how much Terry Lewis knew about what went on in the Licensing Branch.

A couple of days after introducing myself to Allen Bulger, I arrived for my first day at the Licensing Branch. Bulger took me straight to see Detective Inspector Graeme Parker.

DOING THINGS DIFFERENTLY

After we had swapped pleasantries, Parker told me about the nature of the work and explained what was expected of me at the Licensing Branch. He was aware of my policing background and commended me for being a diligent and competent investigator. Then Parker said something that started alarm bells ringing for me: 'We know you have a reputation as a keen and productive worker. However, here we do things a little differently to the way you may have been used to working elsewhere.'

I hadn't been at the Licensing Branch for more than an hour but already I had a sinking feeling in my gut. I asked Parker what he meant by doing things differently.

He weighed up the question for a few moments before answering. Then he replied, 'It's like this, Col. Before you go arresting anyone, when and wherever the occasion may arise, you'll report here and run it by Detective Senior Sergeant Bulger, myself or whoever may be acting in charge of the branch at the time.'

Even though I knew about the corruption at Innisfail, what Parker had just told me still came as a shock. In case I was wondering whether this was just an isolated arrangement, Parker quickly put me straight. The procedure he had just explained to me, he said, was an unwritten and long-standing policy within the Licensing Branch and one which all members working there were required to adhere to. He went on to say that every member of the Licensing Branch had been given the same induction as me and they had all willingly accepted and were prepared to work to the policy he had just outlined.

I wasn't happy and I was pretty certain that Parker would have been able to read it on my face. The tension was palpable and I know he sensed my resistance when he asked me if I had understood his message. I told him that I understood but added that I was sure circumstances would arise when I would need to use my own judgement to make an arrest without referring back to him or Bulger. His annoyance was clear and he didn't speak again but dismissed me with the cold-eyed stare he used on anyone who wouldn't immediately bow to his will.

It soon became clear that I was not the only one having doubts about the move. Kevin Gunthorpe, superintendent-in-charge of the Northern Region up at Townsville, had known my father since the late 1940s, when Kevin was a young constable in Caloundra. He rang me and said, 'Col, whatever possessed you to put in for a transfer to the Licensing Branch? That's certainly no place for you. Most of that bunch are on the take. They'll see you as a threat and they won't hesitate to fix you up if you get in their way. You should get out of there as soon as you can.'

What Kevin was telling me was true, but it was too late. The commissioner had approved my transfer and there wasn't much I could do now except ride it out. Besides, I thought, there had to be some honest police in the Licensing Branch. They couldn't all be corrupt.

Another friend who contacted me was Dudley Orchard. Dudley and I had trained together as probationary constables. We were sworn in and took our Oath of Office together on 31 March 1965. Dudley was convinced there was a sinister motive for my transfer. He said, 'They're using you, Col. They want an honest bloke like you in there so that the rest of the force won't think the whole squad is crook.'

I had to tell Dudley that transferring to the Licensing Branch was my idea, not theirs. But what he said made sense. Was that why they had been so quick to approve my transfer?

FOUR

Licensing Branch

I arrived on transfer to the Licensing Branch from the Brisbane Regional Task Force on 18 October 1982. My first assignment from Parker was to 'police' the massage parlours and escort agencies. I undertook the task with Parker's words about doing things 'differently' ringing in my ears.

It soon struck me that the female workers in the massage parlours were not the slightest bit inhibited by the presence of police. I found it disturbing that some of my men appeared to have more of a social than a professional relationship with the girls.

I got the distinct feeling that the massage parlour receptionists knew about our visits before we arrived. My suspicions were confirmed when one of my officers informed me that Detective Senior Sergeant Harry Burgess (aka 'Dirty Harry') regularly tipped off Ann Marie Tilley, the de facto wife of brothel owner and heroin dealer Hector Hapeta, about impending raids by the Licensing Branch. Burgess would offer the same service to the principals of other massage parlours that operated independently of the Hapeta/Tilley organisation.

Years later it would emerge that Burgess's real role within the Licensing Branch was to oversee all areas of illegal operations—massage parlours, escort agencies, SP betting, pornography, sly grogging, unlawful gaming etc.—to ensure that 'business' ran smoothly and that, in return for the large sums of money they were paying, the people running the rackets were 'looked after'.

At first it puzzled me that Parker never seemed to question or monitor how evidence was being obtained or to make sure that correct procedure was being used to obtain evidence of prostitution. But I soon realised they had a system going. Each of the girls was 'booked' once every four or five weeks. At the Commission of Inquiry it was described as 'booking by arrangement'. The details would all be kept back at headquarters. The officers would know from the records when a particular girl was due for booking or for write-up. It was all very methodical. Sometimes a girl might say, 'Just a minute, Sergeant. I got done a couple of weeks ago. It's not my turn.' If there was a dispute the officer would look it up in the records.

During my first week policing massage parlours and escort agencies, I was sent to check on a massage parlour called Fantasia. This, I discovered, was the centrepiece of the Hapeta/Tilley chain of brothels. It was strategically located in Logan Road, opposite the Gabba cricket ground and less than 100 metres from the busy Woolloongabba Police Headquarters and CIB.

I was surprised to hear the receptionist greet me by my first name, Col. Usually I welcomed warm greetings but this time it felt inappropriate and (for obvious reasons) I was anxious for it not to be misconstrued.

I always treated parlour and escort workers with respect and never judged them, since I knew that many of the women were not there by choice. Some had been deserted by their partners or were victims of domestic violence, some just needed the money to provide for their children. Others were illiterate and simply couldn't find other work. Once there, some of them became trapped by their drug addictions. Receptionists and parlour girls were under strict instructions to deny any knowledge of illicit drugs, but it was no secret that Hapeta and others supplied the girls with heroin.

It wasn't long before I saw evidence of the illegal drugs that were being moved through the massage parlours. Many of the girls working the parlours were clearly under the influence of drugs. The presence of drugs created an added risk for everyone, and their dilated and glassy eyes and slurred speech seemed to make their fellow workers uneasy. In truth they had little to fear, since the likelihood of being arrested for drug use in the parlours ranged from slight to non-existent.

From time to time during the course of my inquiries I would hear the name 'John the Jeweller' or 'the jeweller man'. I would ask my men if they knew who this person was or what he was up to, but they would invariably deny any knowledge of him. It was not uncommon, though, while I was in the parlours to hear one of the girls say, 'Lucy, John the Jeweller was looking for you,' but he had the happy knack of always being just ahead of us, or behind us.

One night, however, I deliberately changed the time of my visit. I went to Fantasia and, as I walked in, I saw a man kneeling over an open briefcase. I recognised him straight away as John Leslie Price (aka John the Jeweller and John McKinnon). He had first come to my attention while I was stationed at Toowong. Price had told me of his years as a heroin addict and pusher in Sydney and said he had come to Brisbane to start a fresh life. He was trying to launch his own advertising business. Occasionally he supplied me with information about the drug trade, which I would pass on to the drug squad. At some point he was picked up on an outstanding warrant from New South Wales and extradited there to serve a prison sentence. But now he was back in Brisbane.

'Hello, John,' I said. He curled away from me with his head in the briefcase. I said, 'John, it's me, Sergeant Dillon.'

He looked very sheepish.

I asked, 'What are you doing here, John?'

He said, 'It's cool. I'm legit. I'm selling jewellery. You can look for yourself.'

I told him it was no good me examining the jewellery as I couldn't tell a piece of glass from a diamond. He told me he was just out of prison and had a job and was going straight, but I didn't believe him. Knowing his background, I examined the briefcase. His car was outside. We searched that as well but could not find any evidence of drugs. I let him go but warned him not to enter the parlours again. It was only a day or two later that one of my men came to me and said, 'Sergeant, guess who's been busted for drugs?' When I told him I didn't know, he said, 'The jeweller man.' I found out that the drug squad had raided his home at New Farm and found a large sum of money, which they said was the proceeds of trafficking drugs. In the end he got about six years.

I found it disturbing that the police showed no interest whatsoever in pursuing illicit drugs in and around the parlours and escort agencies. I had a personal abhorrence of illicit drugs and a loathing for the dealers who sold them, yet I saw evidence on almost a daily basis that drugs were being used and dispensed in those places with impunity. I felt compromised, and it haunts me to this day. But it was too soon for me to take action on my own. I knew that in order to stay in business the drug dealers must have powerful protectors. I had only been in the job a few weeks and was still working out the lay of the land and trying to identify which of my colleagues were honest and which were corrupt.

LICENSING BRANCH

I needed an ally and fortunately I found one. Detective Senior Constable Gary Eric Newman was in his mid-thirties, smart and outgoing and with a warm sense of humour, a quality that was sadly lacking in the Licensing Branch. I put much of this down to Parker, who had created a toxic and suspicious environment that seemed to suit him well. Some were receiving payments over and above their wages while others weren't, and only Parker and perhaps one or two others would have known who fell into which category. It was no wonder rumour and paranoia ran wild.

Gary was one of the few I felt I could trust. His rank at the time, detective senior constable, allowed him to mix more freely with the others in the branch than I could as a sergeant. He was personable but careful, and was a shrewder detective than some of his colleagues gave him credit for. His ability to recall conversations he had overheard in the brothels and parlours was a source of invaluable intelligence about how those businesses were being run.

***

In order to stay on top of the information that was coming in, I regularly reviewed the duty sheets and reports that were supposed to be completed after every shift by each sergeant in charge of a squad. These gave a summary of the duties carried out on each shift, including any breaches or arrests made.

I was sitting at my desk one day when Harry Burgess walked up to me. After looking around to see that no one else was in earshot, he said, 'In your visits to the parlours, have you ever seen anything to indicate that drugs are being used by the girls working there?'

The question startled me. I had already begun making discreet inquiries on the subject with a couple of the girls who I knew were not doing drugs. Why was Harry Burgess asking me about it? Had someone in the parlours tipped him off that I was asking questions or was it just a stab in the dark?

I tried not to be paranoid but in the Licensing Branch paranoia was in the air we breathed.

As calmly as I could, I told Burgess, 'No, I haven't seen anything to suggest drugs are being moved through the parlours.'

He nodded and said, 'That's exactly what I thought. I've never seen anything either.'

As he walked away I told myself that either Harry Burgess was as dumb as an ox (which I knew he wasn't) or he was an unmitigated liar.

***

I suspected that I was being watched. It wasn't long before I knew it for certain.

Cindy—one of the girls I had been speaking to—had warned me that I was going to be taken off the parlours. A few days later I checked the roster and found that, just as Cindy had predicted, I had been moved from parlour duties to policing the SP bookmaking industry.

By now I had started to question my judgement in transferring to the Licensing Branch. It was plain that Parker, Burgess and Bulger had compromised their oath of office as police officers, but how much further did it go? To what extent were they and others actively involved in unlawful activities and who were they protecting?

It was always the girls who were booked, never the owners. Parker and Burgess saw the sheets; they vetted the files. If they had been doing their jobs properly, one of them should have said, 'The girls are being arrested all the time, what about the owners? How about we get our act together and bring in the owners?' But that never happened.

It irked me that Parker hadn't even bothered to speak to me before moving me off parlour duties. Obviously the brothel owners hadn't appreciated me asking questions and they had asked Parker to do something about it. It was

LICENSING BRANCH

becoming clear to me that he and some others in the Licensing Branch were simply doing the bidding of the people running the sex industry.

When I casually mentioned my change of duties to Bulger, Parker's second-in-charge, he told me that it was normal procedure to move the sergeants around so that they could gain experience in all areas of Licensing Branch work. I was careful not to show my annoyance but it made me even more determined to find out how far the corruption went.

SP betting has been around since before I was born and many consider it to be a colourful part of the Australian culture. A well-known politician was reputed to have said it was un-Australian to gaol an SP bookie. But people who like to think of it as a victimless crime probably haven't had much to do with the punters who get beaten up when they can't settle their debts. Most prominent SP bookmakers are known to retain persuasive debt collectors who are never short of work. I've known families who struggled to feed themselves because 90 per cent of the wages went to pay the bookie's debt.

But going after the SP bookies was harder than it looked. The trouble, as I quickly found out, was that they were often well connected, with powerful friends and protectors. Since they usually ran their businesses from pubs and clubs, they were assured of many loyal customers, close at hand, who were eager to shield them from the law.

My first target was a man who combined his day job as a successful businessman with a sideline as an SP bookie. The tip-off came from an informant whose son-in-law was heavily in debt to the bookie. He gave me the bookie's address and warned me that the man had an elaborate security system that included heavy iron grille security doors and bars on most windows.

The house, from which he ran his SP operation on Saturdays, was a sprawling old Queenslander in an upmarket suburb of Brisbane. There were prominent signs outside for both his businesses. Over a period of a couple of weeks I carried out surveillance on the house to make sure that I had the right address. On my activity reports I used the same phrase—'nil activities'—that I had read on dozens of activity reports since joining the Licensing Branch. I made similar entries in my official police diaries. By doing so I was disobeying departmental policy and procedures and putting myself at risk of disciplinary measures by Parker, who was required to make a monthly inspection of all notebooks. But I knew that any intelligence I did disclose would soon find its way to the SP bookie, who would also be tipped off about any impending raid.

I kept a lot of what we were doing secret from other team members, some of whom were reporting my every move back to Harry, who in turn was no doubt keeping Parker fully informed. They were policing me more than the criminals they were being paid to catch.

On the day of the raid I sent one of my team out to make last-minute observations to ensure that the SP bookie's assistant had arrived, indicating that they were getting ready to do business. I planned the raid for mid-afternoon as I knew Parker would have gone home early as he did every Saturday. That would leave either Burgess or Bulger in charge and I knew they would assume that I was heading off with my team to check a list of locations of SP bookmakers given to me by Parker at the start of the shift. Parker always made it clear that we were only to check the places on the list he provided. Since the targets were invariably tipped off in advance, the outcome would always be the same: 'no result'.

The bookie's house was on a main arterial road and entry could only be made via the front gate. A huge brick wall blocked access to the house from the rear. We had to park our vehicles on a busy side road about 100 metres away. What followed next was straight out of the Peter Sellers'

LICENSING BRANCH

movie *The Pink Panther*. Armed with sledgehammers and crowbars, and a search warrant from a Justice of the Peace, we moved along the footpath in single file. If any passing motorist endowed with a good sense of citizenship had called 000, all available police units in the area would have descended on us to prevent what must have looked like a very determined and well-equipped break and enter.

As we approached the house the sound of a radio broadcasting racing results drifted from an open window. The SP bookmaker was sitting with his assistant at the kitchen table, surrounded by betting sheets and telephones. I called out that I had a search warrant and would enter by force if necessary to seize all the instruments of betting on the premises. I gave him a few seconds to think about it. Then I watched him hurry off to open the security door.

As I questioned him about his SP betting activities he tried to pour himself a beer, but most of it was going on the floor. I said to him, 'You're missing the glass,' and he snapped back, 'You're making me bloody nervous, that's why.'

He didn't seem to understand what was happening. After a while he looked up at me and said, 'I've only just finished painting your boss's house.' I thought for a second he must be talking about Parker. Then it dawned on me that he meant the commissioner, Terry Lewis.

After I had finished interviewing the SP bookie and his assistant I asked, 'Do you or your friend have any complaints about the way you have been treated during the course of our visit here today?'

The bookie replied, 'No, in the circumstances you have treated us pretty well. There's no complaints from me.' He turned to his mate and said, 'What about you, Harry?'

Harry shook his head.

I said, 'The next time you're speaking to Commissioner Lewis you can tell him that you had a visit from members of the Licensing Branch and they treated you very well.'

Then I arrested the pair of them and had them taken to the city watch-house to be formally charged with SP betting.

I heard later that the SP bookmaker was in a state of shock and disbelief over his arrest. He told some of his employees—a few of whom were no doubt SP clients as well—that he thought he was safe because he was paying the police for protection. He boasted that during the raid he had been able to hide a big stash of betting slips behind the gas stove. I didn't really mind. Even without the extra slips I felt that we had more than enough evidence to get a conviction.

On the Monday Parker called me into his office. I knew it wasn't so that he could compliment me on a job well done. He was furious but he must have known that there wasn't much he could do. Instead he reminded me that in future all matters that might result in arrests were to be referred either to him or to Bulger for clearance. He gave me that squinty stare of his and asked me whether I had clearly understood his instructions.

I nodded but said nothing.

The SP bookmaker admitted that he had been running his operation for years. He and his mate Harry eventually pleaded guilty to the charge of SP betting and were given heavy fines.

Later I made a check of all the so-called 'activity reports' related to SP betting over the previous couple of years. At least 200 of these reports consisted of a single remark: 'nil activities'.

As a result of the arrests, Parker went to even greater lengths to stop me from disrupting his cosy arrangement with the SP bookies. We continued to be briefed by Parker or Bulger on what our duties and targets for the day would be, but the result was always the same: nil activities and nil arrests.

Every Saturday we would be given a number of locations—usually hotels—where SP betting was supposed to be taking place. We dressed casually and worked in pairs. It soon became obvious that the licensee or duty manager had always been warned to expect me, either by Parker or Bulger or by Harry Burgess, who stayed at the office on Saturdays. As a result of the tip-off, the bookies would either move their operations to another hotel or else sit tight until I had moved on.

I was becoming increasingly disenchanted with my duties at the Licensing Branch and I felt that Parker was beginning to resent having me there. I realised that if I was going to have any chance of catching and prosecuting the SP bookies, I would have to come up with a way to circumvent the obstacles Parker was putting in my way. But Parker wasn't the only problem.

One Saturday as we were on our way to a hotel on Parker's list, the young detective I was with said, 'We won't have much luck here.'

'Why is that?' I asked.

He said, 'The publican here is a good friend of Commissioner Lewis and he will have been tipped off that we are coming.'

The publican in question was a former high profile rugby league footballer from the early 1960s and was well established in the hotel business.

We had just bought a beer and were seated at an island table which gave us an unobstructed view of the public bar where most SP bookies operated from. It was just after midday and the hotel was quite full but there was no sign of an SP bookie.

It was a hotel in the north-western suburbs that I had never visited before. As always, I scanned the patrons to make sure there was nobody whom I recognised and who might therefore recognise me. If I had spotted someone I knew, I would have given the nod to my partner and we would both have got up and left. When performing covert duties, it was always safer to err on the side of caution. Being given up as a copper in a pub full of strangers is not a comfortable experience.

I had a glass of beer halfway to my lips when a voice bellowed, 'Col Dillon, how the bloody hell are you?' I recognised the face and voice at once. I couldn't believe I had missed him. My worst fear was about to be realised. 'Remember me, Col?' he roared. 'We went to school together in Caloundra. Are you still in the coppers?'

At that moment every conversation in the room seemed to stop. I heard a couple of glasses being knocked over as patrons turned from the bar to see what was going to happen next. Others swivelled on their stools to look at us. I could feel their hostile stares. My partner stood up, as he if was expecting a fight.

'Look here, mate,' I said. 'You've got the wrong fellow. I think you've mistaken me for someone else.'

I remembered him well from our school days, although he was in a lower grade to me. I knew it would be hard to convince him that he had made a mistake. 'Ah, come off it,' he said, 'I'd know you anywhere. All you Dillon boys look alike. I grew up with all of you.'

My partner was still on his feet. It was a dangerous situation for the pair of us. 'Look, mate,' I said, 'you've definitely got me mixed up with someone else. I'm not a bloody copper. In fact, I consider that to be an insult. If it's any of your business I'm a truckie.'

He stared at me for a few seconds. I thought he was going to say something but he didn't. I could tell that he didn't believe me, but what could he do? Finally he shook his head and walked away.

My partner sat down and we quickly finished our drinks in case my former schoolmate changed his mind and came back.

LICENSING BRANCH

Chance encounters like that were every undercover officer's nightmare. They were rare but from time to time they happened. When they did, all you could do was try to tough it out. I knew that bloke would have gone home to his wife and said, 'I saw Col Dillon today and he bloody denied it.' The next time I walked into a hotel, I made sure I double-checked every face at the bar.

***

The Licensing Branch was divided into sections but inevitably there was some crossover between them. While working on SP betting and illegal gaming, you could come across people you had met in the parlours and vice versa.

Towards the end of one evening shift my team and I received a complaint that an upmarket motel in Annerley was suspected of being used by prostitutes. The complainant said that men and women were coming and going at all hours of the day and night and that this was upsetting other guests at the motel.

My men and I arrived at the motel around 10 p.m. and staked out the premises from the car park. From the darkened car we were able to see everyone who entered and left with little risk of being seen. Before long a car swung in from the street. It was travelling at high speed and skidded as it turned into the car park. The windows were open and as the driver slowed down we could hear voices yelling at each other. The man and woman inside the car were having a fierce argument.

A semi-circular drive ran from the road to the rear of the motel. Halfway along the drive, the car stopped and the male passenger got out and slammed the door. The female driver kept the motor running. I got out of the car and moved quickly across the car park towards the driver. As the man walked away, the driver put her foot down and accelerated towards him, knocking him over. I thought I heard a bone snap. The man was on the concrete screaming in pain and trying to drag himself to safety. The woman then reversed her vehicle at speed. I thought she was going to exit the motel but instead she straightened the car, revved the motor and accelerated towards the man. She seemed intent on crushing him against the retaining wall that separated the semi-circular drive from the motel garden. As I was the closest, I broke cover and ran over to him. At the same time I waved my arms in the air and screamed at her to stop the car. She hit the brakes, but I could see she wasn't going to stop in time so I had to throw myself up onto the bonnet of her car.

Fortunately the man managed to roll out of its path. The car stopped short of the wall by inches. If I hadn't hurled myself onto the bonnet and the man hadn't rolled clear, either or both of us could have been seriously injured or killed.

Needless to say, as a result of all the drama, our surveillance operation was blown. Lights came on all over the motel; men and women in various states of undress ran out of motel rooms, jumped into their cars and sped off into the night. Clearly our tip-off had been accurate. The motel's regular houseguests were understandably distressed.

The man suffered a broken ankle. As soon as I had pulled the female driver from the car she started kicking and biting and scratching in an effort to have another go at her male companion. I arrested her for driving a motor vehicle under the influence of liquor, assaulting police and resisting arrest. The next day I charged her with the more serious offence of attempting to unlawfully kill. When her case came to court she was ordered to undergo psychiatric assessment and was later deemed unfit to stand trial.

Several months later, after our usual Saturday briefing from Parker, I set off with a colleague to explore the Redcliffe Peninsula for SP bookie activity. We called into our first pub which was at the southern end of the peninsula and was a known rough spot, frequented by trawler

LICENSING BRANCH

crews and motorcycle gangs. We cautiously scanned the public bar and sat ourselves at an island table.

We had only been there a few minutes when I noticed a man on the far side of the room give me a friendly wave. As he started walking towards us, I noticed that he had a limp. My partner asked anxiously, 'Do you know this guy? Are we in trouble?'

Both of us knew that this was not a pub we wanted to be recognised in.

'I know him,' I said. 'I think we'll be OK. Just stay cool.'

The man reached out and shook my hand. 'Fancy seeing you here,' he said. 'You don't remember me, do you?'

'I remember you, mate,' I said. He was the bloke I had saved from being crushed against a wall by his lady friend at the motel. 'How's the ankle?' I asked.

'It's taking a while to heal,' he said, 'but I'm getting there. Are you working in Redcliffe now?'

'No, mate,' I said. 'We're heading to Caboolture and just stopped in for a quiet drink.'

He said, 'I won't hold you up. I never got a chance to thank you for saving my life. That mad bitch would have killed me.'

'I reckon she might've,' I said.

He offered to buy me a drink but I said we were about to leave. He thanked me again and then limped back to his mate across the room.

I said to my partner, 'We're gone. Our cover's blown. We'll get up in a minute and leave quietly.'

I knew exactly what was going to happen next. The bloke with the limp was going to sit down and tell his mate all about how I had saved his life. His mate would tell someone else at the bar and soon the whole pub would know about it. Sure enough, a few minutes later his mate wandered off to the bar. As he chatted to the barmaid, I noticed her glance in our direction. It was time for us to go. However grateful the man was for what I'd done, I didn't want a bunch of bikies and trawlermen knowing that we were cops.

'Come on,' I told my partner. 'We're out of here.'

As we walked out to the car park, I looked back and saw a couple of men come to the door. My partner glared at me over the roof of the car. 'Just in bloody time,' he said.

FIVE

SP bookies . . . a protected species

The unmarked late-model Holden Commodores we drove, with their two-way radios on the dash, were easily identifiable as police vehicles. If the bookies hadn't already been tipped off that we were coming, they would have known when they spotted the car.

An old mate at Toowong who owned a garage and a small fleet of 1970s hire cars used to rent me his vehicles so that we could be less conspicuous. Naturally I didn't say a word to Parker or to anyone else in the Licensing Branch other than a few trusted colleagues. When we left the office I would sign out a departmental vehicle and drive to Toowong where we would switch to a hire car. Over the years quite a few SP bookies were surprised by what they saw jumping out of an old Valiant sedan.

On Thursday, 16 February 1984 I came to work and was told by Parker that I was to go to Roma, almost 500 kilometres west of Brisbane, to search for an SP bookie who had been operating there for years. (By now I was quite used to the idea that an SP bookie could operate for years and never be disturbed by the Licensing Branch.) Parker briefed me on this occasion with the secrecy of a CIA operation and handed me a report he described as 'highly confidential'. He told me to take one other person with me and to be as discreet as possible.

Parker stressed that he wanted the bookie caught before I returned to the office. I jumped to the conclusion that if Parker was so desperate for him to be arrested, it had to be because he was behind in his pay-offs to police. Parker reiterated that we were to be inconspicuous and not book accommodation but instead hire a two-man tent and pitch it on the outskirts of town. I refused. Winter was around the corner and I didn't intend to freeze for him or for anyone else, especially since I didn't trust this job any more than the others Parker had given me.

Before we left, Parker gave me final instructions: as soon as we arrived we were to telephone the district inspector in charge at Roma and make arrangements for him to meet us a couple of miles out of town for further briefings. As we set out for Roma, I said to my partner, 'This is starting to look like another bullshit job. There must be something big going on in Brisbane this weekend and Parker wants us out of the way.'

Neither of us could see the point of a secret meeting with the inspector in charge to obtain more information. Parker had already given us all the information we needed: our target was not only the district's number one SP bookie but he was also a registered bookmaker and operated legitimately at all race meetings. He was well respected and was considered a bit of a legend throughout the west.

From Brisbane by road was supposed to take around five and a half hours, but in our aging Ford Econovan, it took us eight. We drove straight to the local caravan park and booked a site. The caravan we hired for the weekend was old and decrepit, full of holes plugged with pieces of newspaper. There were bloodstains on the inside walls. We couldn't believe that anybody would hire out a van in such appalling condition—or that anyone except us would have agreed to take it. The only consolation was that we would be in town for just two days.

As instructed by Parker, we made contact with the district inspector and met at a secret location, where he told us precisely nothing that we didn't already know. The real purpose of the meeting now seemed obvious to both of us: Parker wanted him to meet us and find out what we looked like in order to tip off the SP bookie.

'Here we go again,' I said to my partner as we drove back to the caravan site. 'We're being sold out to our target.'

'You're not wrong,' he said. 'It looks like another wild goose chase.'

We carried out surveillance on the target's home but never caught a glimpse of his vehicle. He was said to belong to the local equivalent of the Brisbane Club or Tattersall's. The club's members were mostly wealthy graziers and pastoralists. According to Parker, this was where he ran his SP operation. Parker told us we would need to gain entry to the club, but since it was members-only there was little chance of that.

We dressed casually in order to avoid drawing attention to ourselves. From Friday morning until almost midnight we tried in vain to get a sighting of our target. At first light on Saturday, after shivering through a sleepless night in our bloodstained caravan, we set off again. A big race meeting was scheduled for that day and we decided to look for him there.

True to form, there he was in the betting ring with his bookie's clerk, taking bets from the local punters. He was a tall, hard-looking man, perhaps in his late sixties. I had the feeling he might have worked in his younger days as a shearer or wool-presser.

CODE OF SILENCE

There wasn't much we could do except mingle with the crowd, placing the odd bet, while waiting to see where our target went after the meeting. It was thirsty work and after a while we decided to stop for a drink. As I stood at the bar to order a round, two men in classic country attire—R.M. Williams riding boots, denims and ten gallon hats—sidled up to me. I had never seen either of them before, but that didn't mean they didn't recognise me. I thought about our pointless meeting with the district inspector and wondered whether he had passed on our descriptions. If these two were onto us, we would have to leave. They looked friendly enough, though. In a low voice one of them said, 'We don't mean to be rude, but we noticed you as soon as you arrived. When we saw who you were with, we couldn't believe our eyes.'

'Beg your pardon?' I said.

He leaned closer. 'Donald Sutherland,' he said. 'The guy's a Hollywood legend. Man, what's he doing out here in the sticks?'

I looked over my shoulder. There was Brad sitting by himself. The resemblance had never struck me before, but it was true—with his long hair and neatly trimmed beard he did look a bit like Donald Sutherland.

The two men waited for me to say something, but what the hell could I say? I could hardly tell them Brad was just a policeman. I decided the only thing to do was to play along. I said, 'Don's here scouting locations for his next movie. I can't say any more than that.'

One of the men asked, 'Would it be all right if we asked him for his autograph?'

'Sorry, guys,' I said. 'He's trying to keep a low profile. The last thing Don wants is to be pestered for autographs. He just wants a bit of time to relax.'

'That's fair enough,' the other answered. 'We respect that, but would he mind if we shouted him a drink?'

SP BOOKIES...A PROTECTED SPECIES

'Let me check with him,' I said. 'If I give you the nod then it's OK. I can tell you he's rapt in our XXXX beer.'

I returned with our drinks to where Brad was sitting and quickly told him what had happened. 'Mate,' I said, 'you'll have to say yes. You owe it to your fans.'

'If you say so, Sarge,' said Brad.

That put paid to the operation. After Brad's brush with fame, it wasn't safe for us to hang around. We drank our beers and left.

After all the trouble I had given him in Brisbane and the Gold Coast, I assumed that Parker wouldn't be bothered by our failure to make an arrest in Roma, but when we got back to Brisbane he made a big fuss about it. I explained that the only time we had seen the SP bookie was when he was operating legally at the race meeting. It was obvious to me that the reason we hadn't caught the bookie was that he'd been warned we were coming.

***

On Australia Day 1984 two of us were briefed by Parker and Bulger to attend a sports carnival at Carrara on the Gold Coast. The carnival was to include events such as foot races and wood chopping. Some of the best amateur sprinters in Australia would be competing and Parker reckoned the races would attract the attention of the local SP bookies. Our instructions were to hang around the carnival and keep our eyes open. I thought he must be joking, as no SP bookmaker in his right mind would have considered running a book at a public sporting event. Parker's final advice was, 'There's no need for you to go to the Benowa Tavern. Just confine your activities to the sporting event. That should keep you busy enough.'

We drove off to pick up the Valiant hire car at Toowong. In our plain clothes we knew we would fit right in.

I had read plenty of activity sheets relating to the Benowa Tavern: they always reported 'nil activity'. Everyone knew that the Gold Coast was a hotbed of SP betting activity, yet mysteriously the bookies remained untouched. During the 1970s all the local SP bookies operated out of Coolangatta. They would phone their bets across the border to their New South Wales counterparts in Tweed Heads in order to circumvent the racing and betting laws in Queensland.

The notorious 1974 Southport Betting Case had lifted the lid on SP betting and police corruption on the Gold Coast. A number of high-ranking police officers were alleged to have fabricated evidence in order to clear two SP bookmakers from prosecution. This led to the Lucas Inquiry in 1976, but neither the bookies nor the corrupt police were ever convicted. A decade later SP bookmakers were still a protected species in this part of the world.

By the time we arrived at the complex the sports events were well under way. There was already a big crowd. I said to the young detective with me, 'Nothing's going to happen here. We're wasting our time.'

He didn't say anything but I could guess what he was thinking. He was a nervous sort of bloke and I knew he had a great fear of going to court to give evidence on defended matters. In my view he wasn't really cut out for police work at all. I said, 'We'll see if there's anything going on at the Benowa Tavern.'

He turned pale as a sheet and said, 'Inspector Parker told us specifically not to go there. He'll have a fit if he finds out we disobeyed him.'

'That's not your problem,' I told him. 'It's my decision to go there so I'm the one who'll cop it. Don't you worry about it.'

We arrived at the tavern and parked the Valiant in the car park. The place was packed, which already told me something.

SP BOOKIES... A PROTECTED SPECIES

The Benowa Tavern was a nice place, surrounded by beautifully maintained parks and backing onto a tidal canal that flowed into the Nerang River. It was in the very heart of Kombumerri land where for thousands of years my Aboriginal ancestors had hunted, gathered and fished. As we sat in the car I wondered what those ancestors would have thought of me roaming around my traditional land hunting not for food but for SP bookmakers.

The public bar was so full that the patrons—mostly young and middle-aged men—had spilled outside into the summer sunshine. As we made our way through the crowd I spotted him straight away—a solidly built man around 40 years of age sitting on a stool at the main bar, with what appeared to be a newspaper racing lift-out spread in front of him. The sound of horse racing on the radio was coming from a speaker embedded in the ceiling directly over his head. He might as well have had billboards advertising his presence. He looked completely relaxed as he dealt with the steady flow of punters placing bets.

Surprisingly, we managed to get an island table near him, from which we could easily observe his business. What should we do? I knew I would never get a better chance to arrest him. At the same time, I knew that we were on our own—phoning our Brisbane office for backup was out of the question. Nor could I risk asking for help from other police on the Gold Coast. I'd already picked up that if you were a member of the Licensing Branch in trouble and needing assistance, backup was slow to respond, if it bothered to turn up at all. Some of the Gold Coast police might have been receiving money from the bookmaker and they would have been more likely to sell me out than help me make an arrest.

I stood there for a while studying the crowd. They looked a pretty peaceful bunch and not the sort that would give any trouble. I decided that I would confront and arrest the bookmaker. It would be the most daring arrest I was ever likely to make and if it went wrong we would probably both get a belting and end up in the canal.

Trying to sound more confident than I was, I reassured my young partner that if he followed my instructions to the letter we could pull this off without any problems. I told him to move only on my say-so, which would be a subtle nod of my head. The next race was about to start. I waited until the punters had returned to their seats, then walked calmly to where the bookie was sitting.

At first he was so preoccupied with his betting sheets that he didn't notice me. I leant down close to him so that I could speak quietly without attracting any attention from nearby patrons. I had my police badge cupped and concealed in my right hand. I was about to open my mouth when he said, 'The last race is closed, mate, but you're okay for the next in Doomben.'

At that point I showed him my police badge. When he saw it he almost fell off his stool. 'Is this some kind of joke?' he asked.

I could see he was frightened and I immediately knew I had the upper hand. I said to him, 'I want you to look slowly over your left shoulder and into the car park.' I told him that hiding among the cars was a task force of men ready to come storming in as soon as I gave the signal. I said he had two choices: either leave quietly and avoid any embarrassment, or force me to call in the task force and watch them turn the place upside down.

He thought about it for a second and replied, 'Sure, mate. I'll do it your way. I don't want any trouble.'

My next move was to call over the bar attendant. I immediately identified myself to him and said, 'I need somewhere to speak to this gentleman in private and you will have to accompany me, so can you arrange for someone to relieve you?'

SP BOOKIES... A PROTECTED SPECIES

I could tell he didn't know what was going on. 'Sure,' he said. 'We can go into the lounge. It's empty and you won't be disturbed.'

I glanced at my partner, who nodded and followed me into the lounge. After we had closed the door I warned the barman that he had committed offences under the *Racing and Betting Act 1980* by betting with the SP bookmaker and by permitting him to run his operation on licensed premises. I told him that I could arrest him there and then but in view of his cooperation I would proceed against him later by way of a complaint and summons. After feeding him the same line about the task force waiting in the car park, I told him that I wanted to leave the premises with as little fuss as possible. He said, 'You've got my word. I won't be telling anyone in the bar.'

When I questioned the SP bookie and asked for his name, he admitted that he had been operating his business at the Benowa Tavern for some time. While examining his betting slips we found bets recorded on the back of a political leaflet for Russ Hinze, the local state member who was the Minister for Racing and Betting in the Bjelke-Petersen Government, as well as Minister for Police and Minister for Main Roads.

We left the hotel and walked to the car park, where the SP bookie had parked his late model Mercedes Benz. As we walked through the car park, he kept looking around. Finally he asked, 'Where's your task force? I don't see any of them here in the car park.'

'That's how professional they are,' I said. 'As you kept to your word, there was no need for me to call them. Believe me, that was best for everyone.'

I'm not sure he believed me but in any case he decided not to push the point.

I told him we would be driving in his car to the Southport watch-house where he would be formally charged with acting as an unlicensed bookmaker. The SP bookie couldn't believe his eyes when he saw my partner driving the Valiant. 'Bloody hell,' he said. 'Is that the best the police force can supply you with?'

As far as I was concerned, it had been a good day's work. Two of us had snatched an SP bookie from under the noses of a couple of hundred patrons, many of them clients, without a hint of trouble. The bookie was safely locked up in the watch-house. I drove home feeling pretty pleased with myself. I knew, however, that either Bulger or Burgess would call Parker at home and let him know what had happened during the shift. When he heard what I had done he would be ropeable.

* * *

On Monday morning Parker called me into his office. As soon as I entered he told me to close the door. I knew he hadn't called me in for a friendly chat. 'Take a seat,' he said.

We sat in silence while Parker shuffled through some papers, occasionally looking up from his desk to gaze at me over the top of his glasses. He was up to his old mind games, trying to intimidate me. It was nerve-wracking, but I knew I had done nothing wrong. If either of us had something to answer for, it was him.

Suddenly Parker lurched forward and slammed both his hands on the desk. I did the same. We eyeballed each other from a couple of inches apart. It was a showdown that had been looming since my first day at the Licensing Branch: the black man with no power versus the white man with all the power. It reminded me of the staring competitions we used to have as kids in which the first to blink or smile was the loser. Parker was not to know but I had never lost a childhood stare-off. Parker broke first, lowering his head and pulling back to his side of the desk. I knew that was the last time he would attempt to bully me.

SP BOOKIES...A PROTECTED SPECIES

He said, 'I see you had a busy day on Saturday down the coast.'

'Yes,' I said. 'We picked up some work down there.'

Parker said, 'I distinctly told you to attend the sporting event at Carrara and said there was no call for you to go to the Benowa Tavern. What have you got to say for yourself?'

I thought for a while before answering. I said, 'What are my current duties? What work have you allocated for me and my team to do?'

Parker replied, 'To police the Racing and Betting Act.'

'There's your answer,' I said. 'It would have been a waste of our time hanging around the sports and wood chopping at Carrara. That's the last place you'd go looking for an SP bookie.'

I could see Parker was livid but all he said was, 'That's all for now.'

That afternoon he walked over to my desk and asked me to drive him back to his home at Newmarket. I thought it strange because he usually assigned this task to more junior staff. While being driven home he would often give my officers instructions to pass on to me. They found this embarrassing and knew it was a deliberate attempt by Parker to humiliate me. Parker was a stickler for departmental protocol and always insisted on following the chain of command except in his dealings with me.

It was only a few kilometres to Newmarket. Parker hardly said a word but spent the whole time flicking through the newspaper. I thought there had to be a reason why he had wanted to be alone with me but all he said when I pulled up outside his home was, 'Thanks, I'll see you tomorrow.'

If this was another of his mind games, I wanted him to know I wasn't going to play. As he got out of the car I demanded to know what was going on. I told him I was being given the run-around on every job I was allocated. I'd had a gutful, I said.

It was out of character for me to speak like that to a superior officer, but Parker had it coming. He got back in the car and closed the door. I waited for him to say something. He sat for a while staring out of the windscreen. 'All I can tell you,' he said, 'is that what's going on has been going on a lot longer than you and I have been around.'

Without looking at me, Parker opened the door and got out of the car. I sat there dumbfounded while he walked slowly to his front door. With those few words he had as good as admitted his corruption. Where did that leave me? I knew I was a nuisance to him. Was Parker warning me to back off or was he simply telling me that this is what things were like and there was no point trying to change them?

Nothing happened for a couple of days. Then two of the younger detectives in the office, both of whom I trusted, came to me on the quiet and said, 'We overheard a conversation about you upsetting Inspector Parker by arresting that SP bookie on the Gold Coast at the weekend. Apparently it has caused him a lot of embarrassment.'

'How's that?' I asked.

'The bloke you nicked is one of several who are being looked after by this office as well as by some police on the Gold Coast. That's why Parker told you to stay away from Benowa Tavern. The guy's been working out of the tavern for years and nothing has ever been done about it.'

I knew the two detectives had taken a risk in talking to me and I thanked them.

***

Over the next few months I returned several times to the Gold Coast. On each occasion I was able to pick up information about the activities of SP bookies. Again, I deliberately left this out of the activity reports. As a result of the information I arrested a couple more bookies. Word must have come back to Parker that my team and I were wreaking havoc on

SP BOOKIES... A PROTECTED SPECIES

the SP betting industry down there because one day he sent Bulger to tell me to stay away from the Gold Coast and to concentrate instead on the greater Brisbane area.

I was disappointed to see the Gold Coast operation wound up, but not surprised. My team was having an exceptional run; we had arrested a number of SP bookies, most of whom received hefty fines after pleading guilty to the charges.

I guessed that one of Parker's reasons for reassigning me was that he thought he would be able to keep a closer eye on me if I was in Brisbane. I soon found out that my suspicions were correct.

One day I received information about an SP bookie operating from his home at Deception Bay, about 30 kilometres north of the Brisbane CBD. He was part of an SP betting network that had been running for years.

I sent one of my officers to carry out surveillance on the house and reminded him not to disclose anything in his activity report. When he came to see me at the end of the first day he was pretty agitated. People and cars had been coming and going all day. He'd been observing all this activity through his binoculars. At one point he looked past the house into the scrub beyond and found himself gazing straight into the binoculars of a colleague whom I will call Carey, who was known to be one of Parker's cronies.

I said, 'Parker has found out what we're doing and he's got his personal spy tailing us. We're going to have to move quickly on this one.'

On Saturday morning after Parker's briefing, my team and I gathered at Deception Bay to discuss our plan of attack. Any persons arrested were to be taken to Redcliffe police station where they would be formally charged. We raided the target address with three carloads of police and made several arrests. It was clearly a large-scale betting operation with up to a dozen telephones ringing hot right up until the moment when we seized them.

CODE OF SILENCE

The people we arrested were a husband and wife team together with several relatives whom they employed. At Redcliffe police station I was immediately told that a solicitor had been in touch with the officer-in-charge to request that his clients not be questioned until his arrival. I was pretty amazed to hear this because as far as I was aware nobody had made any phone calls from the time we entered the premises and executed our search warrant until the moment we arrived at Redcliffe police station. (This was before everyone had a mobile phone.) I was still trying to work out how it had happened when there was a telephone call for me. It was the solicitor himself, who turned out to be the SP bookmaker's son. He told me that he had been engaged to act for everyone I had just arrested at the house in Deception Bay. I remember thinking to myself: news travels fast on Parker's grapevine.

I wasn't too bothered by what the solicitor told me, since we had more than enough evidence without having to question them. While waiting for him to arrive, we took them to the watch-house where they were formally charged with a number of offences under the Racing and Betting Act.

Before the day was over my team arrested several others involved in the same SP betting ring. News of the crackdown rippled through the industry. It wasn't long afterwards that a lawyer I knew gave me a friendly warning. He said the word going around was that people were not happy at seeing their SP bookmakers arrested. Many punters, he said, preferred to bet with an SP as they found it more exciting than a bet at the TAB or at the track. I found it hard to believe that a handful of arrests could be causing that much trouble.

The lawyer and I were not close friends but he was somebody I trusted.

'Watch your back,' he said.

SIX

A bottle of whisky

I wasn't worried for my physical safety, but I knew that Parker and his mates had other ways of making life awkward for me. A compromising object placed in my locker, followed by a tip-off to Internal Investigations, and my career would be over: I had seen it happen to others. I couldn't afford to drop my guard.

During 1984 I continued to spend my Saturdays chasing SP bookies—without much success, since Parker generally made sure to warn them I was coming.

One Saturday afternoon I was alone in the office with Harry Burgess. I had finished writing up my duty sheet and was on my way out when Burgess called out from the detective senior sergeant's office, 'Hang on, Col. I want to see you for a moment.' He caught up with me by the water cooler in the corridor. Burgess and I had never had much to say to each other. He must have known that I didn't trust him. I had no idea why he would want to talk to me now. He watched me pour some water from the cooler and drink it. Then he said, 'How would you like to earn some extra money?'

I said, 'What do you mean by extra money?'

He said, 'Four hundred dollars a month and you don't have to do anything for it. All you have to do is not be in certain places at certain times. It can be done real easy. For instance, say you and I happen to pass each other in the corridor—I slip the four hundred into your pocket and nobody is any the wiser. There's no need for you to know who's paying or where it's coming from. No one but you and I will know about it. How does that sound?'

I felt angry, insulted and humiliated by Burgess's clumsy attempt to bribe me, but I tried not to show it. If I hadn't been certain of it before, I knew now that Burgess was bent. He stood there with a gormless look on his face, waiting for me to answer.

I had to say something. 'Look,' I told him, 'I'll need to take some time to think it over.'

'Not a problem,' said Burgess. 'I'll see you next Saturday when we're both working again. In the meantime there's nowhere you can go to about this. It's no good telling the boss. He'll just look at you and wonder what you're on about.'

I didn't need Burgess to tell me not to bother going to Parker, since I knew that Parker had been on the take ever since his time in Innisfail, if not before.

Burgess went back to his office while I walked the kilometre or so to where my car was parked. It was only now that the implications of Burgess's offer began to sink in. I knew that Burgess and Parker and probably Bulger were corrupt but how far up the line did it go? Was it confined to the Licensing Branch and a few corrupt detectives on the Gold Coast or was it bigger than that?

The only person I felt I could talk to was an old friend, retired Regional Superintendent Keith Harris. Keith had been my boss at Newmarket police station in the early 1970s

A BOTTLE OF WHISKY

and I still visited him regularly. I told him what Burgess had said and we spoke about it for some time. As far as Keith was concerned, I had two options: I could go along with Burgess's offer, try to draw him out and expose him for what he was, or I could just say I wasn't interested. I thought about the first but it felt too risky; I just didn't know what was involved or how far it went.

A week later, on the Saturday, I was getting ready to leave the office after my shift when I noticed Burgess. He seemed to be hanging back, as if he wanted to talk to me. I picked up my case and said, 'See you. Goodbye.'

As I walked down the corridor Burgess called out, 'Have you got a minute?'

I said, 'Yes, sure.'

Burgess said, 'Did you consider my offer?' When I hesitated, he said, 'What I spoke to you about last week, about the money.'

I replied, 'Yes, mate. I've thought about it hard and I've decided no. I'll just stay as I am and do my own thing.'

'OK,' he said. 'No hard feelings.'

The matter was never raised again.

Burgess's attempt to bribe me was the clearest evidence yet that I had rattled Parker. I knew that Harry wouldn't have approached me without speaking to Parker first. What would they do once they realised they couldn't buy me off? I didn't have to wait long to find out. A few weeks later I found a bottle of Chivas Regal Royal Salute Scotch whisky in my private locker. It felt to me like a warning: if someone could plant a bottle of whisky in my locker, they could plant other things too. (I found out later that Burgess had delivered it on behalf of Ann Marie Tilley.)

* * *

A short time afterwards I received a request from Parker to see him in his office. We had always kept our distance but recently Parker had been noticeably cooler towards me. I tried to think of any blunders I might have made that Parker could use against me. The combination of Burgess's attempted bribe and the bottle of whisky in my locker was making me nervous.

When I walked into his office Parker said, 'I'm sending you to Mareeba to do a job up there.'

Here we go again, I thought. There must be something pretty important about to happen here in Brisbane and he wants me out of the way. I asked him what the job was.

Parker said, 'I want you to go to Mareeba and see if you can catch a fellow who goes up there every year with a semitrailer loaded with casks of wine which he flogs to the Italians up there. I want him prosecuted for selling alcohol without a licence.'

I stared at him in disbelief. Brisbane and the Gold Coast were steeped in every kind of vice and Parker was sending me to the other end of the state to arrest a bloke for selling a few casks of wine.

He saw the look on my face and said, 'Do you have any problem with going up there to do the job?'

'None at all,' I said. 'Just that it's a long way to go if he doesn't show up. How certain are you that he will be there?'

I could feel him losing patience with me. He said, 'He comes up every year without fail and my information is he's ready to head off any time for Mareeba.'

'Do you have any more details about this person?'

'He travels up from Griffith in New South Wales and his name is Tony Sergi.'

I didn't say anything for a few moments. I knew all about Antonio 'Tony' Sergi (born 29 October 1935). The Woodward Royal Commission into drug trafficking had found that money from the production and selling of cannabis had gone into Tony Sergi's winery and linked Sergi to the cannabis growers in Griffith. These were people who had ordered Donald Mackay's murder.

Knowing that I had spent most of my career in uniform, Parker would have had no inkling that I was aware of Tony Sergi's background. Like many other detectives, Parker tended to look down his nose at uniformed police. He would have expected me to have little interest in and even less knowledge of complex criminal cases like the Mackay murder investigation. (I've never been able to understand that prejudice, since any half-decent detective knows that it is the conscientious and switched-on uniformed officer at the scene of the incident who invariably supplies the information to point the detectives in the right direction— and believe me when I say some need pointing in the right direction!)

I'm sure Parker sensed my apprehension at the mention of Tony Sergi. I had the feeling that I was moving into more sinister territory. I knew that Parker wasn't telling me the whole story.

I should have kept my thoughts to myself but instead I blurted out, 'That's bullshit, this fellow coming all the way from Griffith to sell wine to other Italians. I'd be more interested in what he takes back in the barrels once they're empty—that's if he does bring them up full of wine, which I very much doubt.'

Never at any time in our conversation did I make any reference to drugs.

I went on, 'Italians do not drive halfway across the country to sell wine to other Italians. They all make their own.'

Parker and I had both served in the far north, a place with a large Italian population. He knew that what I was saying about the wine was true. He snapped back, 'What do you mean you'd be more interested in what his return load will be?'

'Exactly what I said.'

I realised I had struck a nerve and suspected that Parker knew there was more to Tony Sergi's Mareeba trip than selling wine. Parker had every opportunity to warn me about Sergi's background but he didn't say a word. Not once did he advise me to proceed with caution and be on my guard when and if I caught up with Sergi. All he said was, 'I'm sending a couple of fellows with you. That should be enough.'

I wasn't happy about Parker deciding who should accompany me to Mareeba and it was no surprise when he nominated two men who were widely regarded as 'Harry's boys'. I knew that they felt no loyalty towards me and I didn't trust either of them. They would not be there to help me but to keep an eye on me and report back to Parker.

I pushed him for more information. 'What sort of primemover and trailer will he be driving? Do we know the make or colour? What's his estimated time of arrival in Mareeba? Is there a particular place where he stays when he's in Mareeba?'

Parker brushed my questions aside and said, 'What I've told you is all the information I have. You'll have to play it by ear. He shouldn't be too hard to find. Just keep a look out for a semitrailer laden with casks and bearing New South Wales number plates.' He paused for a few moments before dismissing me.

I left Parker's office feeling very uneasy. The Mareeba job felt ominous. I wasn't familiar with the town and would once again be working blind, probably with my target already forewarned of my intentions. I faced the usual problem of not knowing whether I could trust the local police.

The next day I was rostered on a day shift. I had only been at my desk a few minutes when Parker walked past my desk and told me that he wanted to see me straight away in his office.

'Close the door and take a seat,' he said.

A BOTTLE OF WHISKY

He got straight to the point. 'About the job we discussed yesterday. I've changed my mind about sending you to Mareeba. I've got a far better job for you which will make you the envy of the office.' As he spoke I could feel him studying my face for any reaction. I gave him nothing. I couldn't wait to hear what the trade-off was for being pulled off the Mareeba job. Parker said, 'I'm sending Greg White and his team to do the Mareeba job and when he's finished there he can join you on the job I'm going to give you and you can come back to the office together.'

Greg was another detective sergeant. Although I had seen him around, I had never met him before coming to the Licensing Branch. Greg was a quiet and unassuming fellow. He struck me as a bit of a loner and didn't appear to socialise with any of the other officers, but he was an honest and capable detective. When Parker decided to give him the Mareeba assignment he was out of the office on another job, so I couldn't contact him, but as an experienced detective he would have known who Tony Sergi was.

Parker said, 'I can't tell you about your new assignment just yet as I'm still working out the details but I'll tell you closer to the time. You'll need to liaise with Sergeant White as to where you'll meet up after he has finished the job in Mareeba.'

I didn't ask Parker why he had changed his mind about the Mareeba job but I didn't have to. After what I had told him, he was smart enough to guess that I wouldn't bother about the wine but would wait for Sergi and intercept him as he was heading back to Griffith with his return load, which I would have staked my reputation would be marijuana destined for sale in Sydney and Melbourne.

Mareeba was right in the heartland of old-time Calabrian mafia activity and was known to be a significant marijuana-growing area with links to Griffith. Over many years, casks used to deliver wine to the area were reported to have been used to transport cannabis south. Later there were rumours that Donald Mackay's body had been buried in a well on a property in Mareeba, but the investigation failed to find any evidence. A number of murders of people connected with the cannabis trade had also been committed near Mareeba. I can't say I was sorry to have been pulled off the job.

***

While Detective Sergeant White and his team went to Mareeba, I was dispatched to investigate allegations of prostitution and unlawful gaming in Mackay and Airlie Beach. The two men who were to have accompanied me on the Mareeba job were now reassigned to the new job—no doubt with the same brief to watch me and report back to Parker.

Before leaving for Mackay I made arrangements with White to meet up in Airlie Beach after he had completed his job in Mareeba. I assumed Parker would have given White pretty much the same briefing as he had given me. I didn't discuss with Greg my views on what I thought the Sergi job was all about, since it was only supposition on my part. In any case, I had my doubts that Sergi would even show up.

The target in Mackay was a local man who was alleged to control prostitution and unlawful gaming in the region. Parker supplied me with the address of the club where the illegal gambling was supposed to be taking place.

Our first task after arriving in Mackay was to carry out surveillance at the address Parker had given us, but this was easier said than done. It was a commercial premises in a busy area that made it difficult to watch without being conspicuous. We soon found out that an escort business was operating as a front for prostitution. There seemed to be no shortage of clients. After keeping the place under surveillance for a couple of nights we obtained a search warrant and went in. As I was questioning one of the women in the kitchen, a bull voice roared out, 'Who the hell do you think you are coming in here? Get off the premises immediately.'

Looking round, I was confronted by a tall, thickset man with forearms like Christmas hams. It went through my mind that he could have lifted me above his head and thrown me out the door and down the steps if he had wanted to (fortunately, he didn't). I told him, 'I am investigating allegations that these premises are being used for prostitution. I have a search warrant that empowers me to enter, search and seize documents, records and anything else that may confirm whether or not any offences have been committed.'

'Look, mate,' he said. 'I'm running a legitimate business here, I take good care of these girls and have them medically examined once a week.' He snatched a handful of medical receipts off the door of the refrigerator and thrust them under my nose.

I told him we had already arrested three of the women and that they were in the process of being charged at the Mackay police station.

'You're wasting your time,' he said. 'Your charges won't stand up in court.'

'That remains to be seen,' I replied.

'I've told you once,' he said. 'Now get out of here.'

Trying not to look at those forearms, I said, 'I've already shown you the search warrant which lawfully authorises us to be here. I'm not leaving until I have finished interviewing these ladies.'

He turned to them and shouted, 'Don't you tell them a bloody thing. They've got nothing on you if you don't cooperate.' I could see the women were terrified of him. There was no way they were going to disobey him by talking to us.

By now I'd had enough of him. I said, 'This is my first and last warning. If you persist in obstructing us in our duty I'll have you arrested and you'll be coming with me to the watch-house.'

'You haven't heard the last of this,' he said as he left. 'You bastards will be hearing from my solicitor.'

It was just as well he hadn't forced me to arrest him as I'd have had a hell of a job taking him into custody if he had resisted. His behaviour towards us made me wonder whether he was being protected by some members of the local police.

As for his supposed gambling operation, the only way we could have got a warrant to search the premises for instruments of gaming would have been by getting an agent inside and having him participate in any unlawful games taking place. There was no chance of that happening, since it would have been impossible to have a complete stranger walk in off the street and be accepted straight up.

***

The Mackay job had netted us a few arrests but as we headed for Airlie Beach I couldn't help feeling that we were going to have trouble making the charges stick.

Airlie Beach, as always, was busy with tourists on their way to or from the Whitsunday Islands. Like many other resorts, it was a magnet for opportunistic drug dealers who hung around the town targeting young people from Australia and overseas.

Greg White and his team arrived on schedule. Greg's mouth fell open when he saw the moderately priced holiday apartment we had rented for our stay. He told us that he and his guys had had to rough it in Mareeba in order not to be noticed. At one spot where they went looking for Sergi, they had found themselves covered in scrub ticks. Greg said they had moved around the area for about a week making discreet inquiries as to whether or not Sergi was in town or was expected to arrive. One of the locals had told him that Sergi wasn't coming, which was unusual since he made the trip pretty much every year. It was clear

A BOTTLE OF WHISKY

to Greg that Sergi was well known in Mareeba. I distinctly remembered Parker telling me, 'He comes up every year without fail and my information is he's ready to head up there any time.' All I could think was that in light of our conversation, Parker had given Sergi a good reason not to come this year.

Parker was right when he said I'd be the envy of the rest of the branch for going to the Whitsundays, but the job itself didn't really amount to anything. It certainly didn't repay the time and effort that had gone into it. To Parker it was probably money well spent to see the back of me for a few days—not that he was likely to admit it. In fact, when he read my report he looked annoyed and said the whole thing had been a fairly costly exercise and we hadn't got much to show for it. I had to bite my tongue and refrain from saying, 'We might have got a better result if the targets hadn't been tipped off that we were coming.'

I did say, 'Greg told me he didn't have any luck in Mareeba. That fellow Sergi never turned up. Strange, isn't it?'

Parker gave me his usual cold stare and said, 'That will be all.'

By now I was certain that Parker wanted me out of the branch. The question was, how to get rid of me?

One morning Parker called me to his office and said, 'I'm taking you off shift work. I want you to look at the Liquor Act and redraft some of the outdated charges.' Was there a smirk on his face or was I just imagining it? He paused before going on, 'This job has needed doing for some time. It should keep you busy for a while.'

So this was how Parker was planning to drive me out of the Licensing Branch. Redrafting laws was not my area of expertise and Parker knew it. If I had wanted to be a desk clerk or write policy I would not have joined the police force. Being taken off shift work would also mean a significant reduction in my pay since I would lose my penalty rates.

CODE OF SILENCE

Parker waited for me to say something. Maybe he was hoping I would protest or even refuse to do the new job, which would have given him the justification he needed to kick me out. But I had no intention of making things easy for him. I saw exactly what he was up to but I had no valid reason to argue. I was pretty sure I would hate the job but I knew I could stick it out in the event Parker's ploy backfired. A young detective whom I liked and trusted, and who was studying to practise law, offered to help me redraft the charges. We followed Parker's instructions to the letter. The job took less than a fortnight, leaving me once again with nothing to do.

SEVEN

The code

Parker called me into his office and told me I was back on the roster. He said, 'There's a new nightclub called Pharaoh's started up in Adelaide Street. The word is that it's unlicensed and taking a lot of trade away from licensed premises in the area. I want you to find out who's running the place and take the necessary action to close it down.'

It was a typical Parker briefing: no names, just hearsay masquerading as intelligence. There was no doubt in my mind that Parker would have known exactly who was operating those premises and the nature of the business going on there, but he had no intention of sharing that information with me. In this case he didn't have to, because I knew from my own sources that Pharaoh's was one of the clubs owned by Hector Hapeta and Ann Marie Tilley, Brisbane's king and queen of vice. I didn't tell Parker I knew, but I couldn't help wondering why he wanted the place closed down, since Hapeta and Tilley were paying for police protection.

I could only draw the conclusion that they were not paying enough.

The usual modus operandi for raids by the Licensing Branch on places like Pharaoh's was that staff at the club would receive a tip-off before the police arrived which would enable them to move their liquor stocks out of harm's way until the raid was over. The managers were under firm instructions to leave a small amount of stock on the premises to be confiscated by police. To the uninformed, this gave the impression that the raids were genuine efforts on the part of police to clamp down on illegal activities. What they didn't know was that as soon as the police had left, the premises would immediately be restocked and it would be business as usual. The small quantities of liquor confiscated were supposed to be lawfully disposed of under 'strict supervision' or else forfeited to the Crown for on-selling to railway refreshment rooms throughout Queensland.

It wasn't difficult to confirm that Pharaoh's nightclub belonged to Hapeta, since the women who worked there also worked in massage parlours and escort agencies operated by Hapeta and Tilley. It was common knowledge that liquor and sex were available at Pharaoh's for a price.

Pharaoh's opened for business around 11 p.m., when licensed premises had to close their doors under the terms of the Liquor Act. (Naturally there were places that, with a nod from the police, continued serving drinks long after the permitted trading hours!)

Before raiding Pharaoh's I needed to be sure what was going on inside, so I asked one of the few officers I trusted to go undercover and report back to me. He quickly confirmed that liquor of all kinds was being sold and that prostitutes were openly serving customers on the premises. He saw no evidence of illegal drugs but I had strong suspicions that they were available to those in the know, and were perhaps being sold behind the scenes to the girls who worked there.

THE CODE

It was about mid-afternoon the next day when my team and I descended on Pharaoh's. I had no trouble obtaining a search warrant. As luck would have it, our arrival coincided with the delivery of a large consignment of beer. We found piles of beer cartons in a back room. Altogether there must have been a few thousand dollars' worth of alcohol on the premises.

The manager was a softly spoken man in his forties. He was courteous but determined not to cooperate. I began by asking him who owned the premises. He told me he didn't know. I then asked him the name of the lessee; again he said he didn't know. When I asked him what his position was at the club, he answered that he was the manager. He refused, however, to tell me the name of his employer, or of the person he was answerable to.

The conversation was becoming more ridiculous with every question I asked. I wondered whether it was fear or loyalty that made him refuse to cooperate and concluded that it was probably the latter. He belonged to the school that said you don't break the code of silence or give anyone up, particularly to the authorities—a code, strangely enough, that he shared with many of my colleagues in the police.

I asked him who paid him his wages and he said he didn't know. I asked him how he received his pay: was it in cash or by cheque? He told me that he was paid in cash and that his pay was delivered by courier. Who sent the courier? He didn't know.

I told him that I had information that the club was owned by Hector Hapeta jointly with Ann Marie Tilley but he claimed never to have heard of them.

Finally I decided I'd had enough. Patience was always a virtue when questioning a potential suspect, but mine had run out. I told him I was going to carry out a thorough inspection of the premises and he would have to accompany me. We went into his office and as I looked around I noticed a black briefcase on the floor resting against a four-drawer filing cabinet. I asked him to open the filing cabinet, which proved to be empty. I was hoping to find documentation of some kind—invoices, for example—to indicate who owned or was leasing the property.

I picked up the briefcase and asked the manager if it belonged to him. He said it didn't belong to him and that he didn't have a clue who owned it or how it came to be in his office. He sounded a bit nervous. The briefcase was locked with a combination lock. I told him it was somebody's property and asked him what steps he had taken to try and find the lawful owner.

'None,' he said. 'As I said before, I don't even know how it came to be in here.'

'Are you telling me,' I said, 'that you're the manager of these premises, this is your office and you don't know how this briefcase came to be here?'

'That's right,' he said. 'I haven't a clue.'

I said, 'Let me make it quite clear to you what the situation is with this briefcase: either it is lost property or stolen property or it can be reasonably suspected of being stolen in the absence of its lawful owner.'

He must have thought I was pulling his leg, but I was being deadly serious because the briefcase was the only leverage I had to persuade him to cooperate.

I said, 'We need to find out the owner of this briefcase and to make sure that it is returned. As it was found by me here in your office, I'm going to need you to open it in my presence to see if it contains anything to indicate who it belongs to.'

He asked, 'Is it lawful to do this?'

It seemed a pretty funny thing to be asked by a man who was going to be charged with managing an unlicensed club which sold liquor and had prostitutes on the premises.

I replied, 'Yes, in the circumstances it is.'

THE CODE

He went looking for a screwdriver and used it to break open the briefcase.

There was nothing in the briefcase except a bound foolscap book. The pages had been neatly ruled into columns. One column consisted of a list of names: Monique, Fifi, Giselle, Angel etc. Another showed an amount of money beside each name. There were various references to jewellery. I didn't have to be Einstein to work out that the names were pseudonyms for women working as prostitutes. The money evidently corresponded to purchases—although I seriously doubted they were buying jewellery. I kept turning over the pages until I reached a blank page with a note that made my hair stand on end. It was legible but written in a shaky hand that made me suspect the writer was high or intoxicated. The note said:

> Lisa will help you sort out this mess. Sorry it comes to you at a bad time. I just got mixed up in the heroin again. It is quite a disease. Please give Lisa a chance as she has about 300 clients and ready access. She can write up as much as myself with a little training and guidance from yourself—thanks mate.

I knew that Lisa was a pseudonym used by Hector Hapeta's de facto wife and business partner, Ann Marie Tilley, and I had a strong suspicion the account book—and briefcase too—belonged to my old friend John the Jeweller, aka John Leslie Price and John McKinnon.

We returned to the office with several thousand dollars' worth of alcohol, accompanied by the far from happy manager of Pharaoh's. The amount of grog we delivered to the exhibit room raised plenty of eyebrows and had the office buzzing.

***

It wasn't long before Parker called me to his office and asked me what had happened at Pharaoh's. I told him I had obtained a search warrant before raiding the premises and that we had confiscated a large consignment of beer and spirits. Parker said, 'Did you find out who owns the premises or who's running it?'

I said, 'No. We brought the manager in and he won't cooperate. He says he hasn't got a clue who owns or runs it, but my information is that it is run by Hector Hapeta and Ann Marie Tilley.'

Since joining the Licensing Branch, I had only ever seen and spoken to Tilley once and I had never laid eyes on Hapeta, who was reputed to keep a low profile, leaving the business side of things to Tilley. I remembered very clearly being told by some of the younger detectives when I first arrived at the Licensing Branch that Tilley and Hapeta were untouchable and were never to be questioned in relation to their massage parlour and escort operations. They had also warned me about a premises at 142 Wickham Street, Fortitude Valley that was a no-go area for Licensing Branch police as it was an 'unofficial' casino said to be owned and run by Geraldo Bellino and Vic Conte, who were supposed to have been given the green light by senior police. There were said to be regular business meetings between the Bellino syndicate and Hapeta and Tilley in the basement of a massage parlour called Bubbles Bath-House.

After raiding Pharaoh's and confiscating a large quantity of alcohol, my next step was to find Hapeta and Tilley and interview them both about the ownership of the club. I was fairly certain that Parker would not want this to happen.

It seemed a good moment to tell him about the briefcase and my suspicion that John the Jeweller was in collusion with Hapeta and Tilley to push drugs through the massage parlours.

THE CODE

After listening to what I had to say, Parker told me to give my information to the Drug Squad.

I said, 'The Drug Squad know all about John the Jeweller. In fact they have charged him with a number of serious drug offences and he is either awaiting trial or sentence.'

'Nevertheless,' said Parker. 'What you have just told me is additional information.'

I noticed that he had taken great care not to mention either Hapeta or Tilley. His only concern seemed to be John the Jeweller. I didn't mind going to talk to the Drug Squad, although I didn't think I would be telling them anything they didn't know already. But I had no intention of letting Hapeta and Tilley off the hook. I said to Parker, 'Everything points to Hapeta being the owner of Pharaoh's, so I'm going to have to interview him. I've heard it said inside the branch that Hapeta and Tilley are untouchable, so what's the go here?'

I could see he was annoyed and guessed that he was already working out a way to white-ant my inquiries. He said, 'You can interview Hapeta. But first I want you to go to the Drug Squad and tell them what you know about this John the Jeweller.'

The Drug Squad was in a building across the street, a few minutes' walk away. I arrived at the front counter and pressed the service bell. A senior detective whom I didn't know by name but had seen around came to the counter. I had the distinct impression that he had been waiting for me. He was about the same age as Parker and I wondered whether the two of them had worked together. Parker must have jumped on the phone as soon as I was out of the office and told him I was coming over.

I started to tell him about the briefcase and accounts book that I had found in the manager's office but he wasn't really interested in what I had to say. He gave the book a cursory glance and said it wasn't much to go on. I left the Drug Squad feeling that I had been fobbed off.

When I got back to the Licensing Branch, Parker was waiting for me. He said, 'The owner of that briefcase has phoned here looking for it and he's coming in from Mt Gravatt within the next half hour to collect it.'

I asked, 'Did he give his name?'

Parker said the caller had given a name but it wasn't the name of the man we knew as John the Jeweller.

I didn't think John the Jeweller would be stupid enough to collect the briefcase in person; he would send one of his associates. But I told Parker it would be worth putting a tail on whoever collected the briefcase since there was a chance it might lead us to Hapeta or to John the Jeweller's supplier.

Parker didn't even bother responding to my suggestion. It was clear that he had no intention whatsoever of putting in a request for the person collecting the briefcase to be followed. He said, 'The owner is coming in to collect his briefcase and you'll see that it's returned to him. Have him sign an indemnity receipt and file it in our office records.'

I said, 'What about the book?'

Parker said, 'It's his lawful property and you have no power to hold onto it.'

I knew I'd be wasting my time trying to persuade Parker to have the owner of the briefcase followed. All I could do was cut my losses. I said 'Someone else can deal with the briefcase and get a receipt for it. I'm taking one of my men and heading out to Hapeta's place to interview him about Pharoah's.'

Before leaving the office I took the accounts book out of the briefcase and unbeknown to Parker (or anyone else in the Licensing Branch) made several photocopies of the pages containing the girls' names and the sums of money they owed. At the end of my shift I took the photocopies home with me

THE CODE

and later on gave a copy to a trusted friend with instructions to look after them. In the event of anything untoward happening to me, he should produce them to some competent and lawful authority to affirm my belief that drugs were being channelled on a large scale through the Hapeta/Tilley brothels.

Hapeta and Tilley shared a neat weatherboard cottage in Hill Street, Spring Hill. We parked directly outside. Before I could get past the gate, the front door swung open and Tilley bid us a cheery welcome. Harry Burgess was said to have a close relationship with Tilley and I assumed that Burgess had warned her that I was on my way.

Tilley invited us inside. Hapeta was waiting for us in the living room. He was a gigantic man—I estimated he weighed between 160 and 190 kilograms—and was sitting behind a large office desk. During the entire interview Tilley stood close to Hapeta with her hand on his shoulder. He looked far more anxious than she did, which seemed ironic given his enormous size.

Before we started the interview I casually asked Tilley how she happened to open the front door at the very moment we came through the gate. She smiled and pointed to a closed circuit TV monitor in the corner of the room which showed all the traffic entering their street from both ends. Given the kind of people they rubbed shoulders with, it didn't seem necessary to ask why it was there.

Hapeta wasn't much of a talker and answered mostly in grunts and monosyllables. I noticed he began to perspire profusely. When I asked him about his connection with Pharaoh's, he admitted the club belonged to him and said it had only recently opened for business. There were a few times when I thought he was going to dry up on me altogether but Tilley would always step in and give him a prompt. I was about to ask him the most obvious question—whether or not he had a licence for the sale of liquor—when he announced that he planned to apply to the Licensing Commission for a licence so that he could operate within the law. It crossed my mind to tell him that he should have considered that before but I thought it might upset him!

I certainly found his behaviour puzzling. Tilley was as cool as a cucumber but Hapeta was a bag of nerves. The pair of them had been running brothels and paying off the police for years, yet Hapeta seemed as flustered as a first-time shoplifter.

As we talked, I noticed a leather briefcase sitting on top of a metal filing cabinet behind Hapeta's desk. It looked similar in shape, size and colour to the one I had found at Pharaoh's, which I suspected had been left there by John the Jeweller on one of his visits to sell 'jewellery' to the girls.

'Hector,' I said, 'that's a nice-looking briefcase you have behind you. It reminds me of one that belongs to a fellow named John the Jeweller.' I paused before asking, 'Do either of you know anyone of that name?'

Hapeta's whole body started to shake. His breath came in gasps. Tilley's air of imperturbability vanished and she took her hand off Hapeta's shoulder. 'You'll have to excuse me,' she said. 'I need to go next door for a minute. I won't be long.'

'No problem,' I said. 'We'll stay here with Hector.'

Hector looked as if he was going into shock. For a while I was worried that we might have to call an ambulance for him. Then Tilley hurried back into the room. She said. 'I've just been on the phone to our solicitor and he told me that we do not have to answer any more questions.'

She was right, of course. They were not under any legal obligation to answer any of our questions. She also had the right to ask us to leave. To judge by their reaction, it was clear that both Hapeta and Tilley were well acquainted with John the Jeweller and his business.

I didn't for a second believe that it was Tilley's solicitor who had advised her not to speak to us. My guess was that she had made a phone call to the Licensing Branch and that it was Harry Burgess who had told her not to cooperate.

THE CODE

Later that day I told Parker that Hapeta had admitted to running Pharaoh's nightclub and that I intended to have him prosecuted for breaches of the Liquor Act. To my surprise, Parker more or less assented to it. I didn't tell him that I'd also tried to question both Tilley and Hapeta about John the Jeweller because I knew that he would have heard about it from Burgess.

A week or so later Parker came over to my desk and said, 'You're getting close to your next promotion, Sergeant, but if you don't pull your horns in it might not happen.' I immediately stepped out from behind my desk and we stood face to face, eyeballing one another. It was a threat he should never have made. I took it as proof of the pressure he was coming under from the people he was supposed to be protecting from prosecution. As we stood there inches apart I half wondered if Parker was expecting me to throw a punch, but if that was what he was thinking he had misread me. I said, 'You're right, Inspector. I am close to my next promotion and I certainly don't fit in here at the Licensing Branch. But the only way for you to get rid of me is to make sure I get that promotion.' Parker turned away and headed for his office.

That confrontation was to be our last. In a few months my promotion to sergeant first class came through and I was gone from the Licensing Branch.

EIGHT

The black cat

My promotion and transfer to the Police Operations Centre on 23 August 1984 happened so quickly that I thought Parker must have engineered it himself. It certainly suited both of us.

The operations centre wasn't my idea of a dream transfer, but anywhere would have been a relief after the Licensing Branch. I was mentally and physically exhausted and I knew it would give me the chance to recharge my batteries before returning to operational policing.

The officer-in-charge was Superintendent Terry McMahon, a warm and cheerful man who had served most of his career in the Criminal Investigation Branch (CIB). I had a lot of respect for Terry and enjoyed working for him. I was less enamoured with his second-in-charge, Inspector Darcy Buckley, who had been transferred from the Brisbane Crime Intelligence Unit, where he had been the officer-in-charge. During my time at the Licensing Branch I had often seen

Buckley visiting Parker in his office. Their meetings always took place behind closed doors. I had no reason to believe that there was anything other than a professional relationship between the two, but my low opinion of Parker rubbed off on Buckley. I didn't trust Parker and I found it hard to trust anyone who had anything to do with him.

I hadn't been at the Police Operations Centre for long when Terry McMahon was elevated to the rank of assistant commissioner. His promotion left a vacancy for the position of superintendent of the operations centre and I was keen to discover who would take his place.

One day I was walking along the pavement outside headquarters when I bumped into two former colleagues from the Licensing Branch. 'Col,' one of them said, 'you must have run over a black cat.'

The look on my face must have made it clear that I didn't know what he was on about.

The two of them looked at each other. Then the other said, 'You're getting your old boss back. Parker has just been promoted to superintendent and is going to the operations centre. You'll both be together again.'

I couldn't believe it. I didn't think Parker would be any happier with the situation than me, but as my superior officer he would be in a position to make life a lot harder for me than I could for him.

The first thing Parker did was to call me to his office and tell me he was taking me off shift work, just as he had when he was my boss at the Licensing Branch. For a man who had spent half his career on the take, he knew how to hit you where it hurt—in the hip pocket. He told me he had a special project for me: I was to work on developing counter-disaster plans for the city of Brisbane. Until now, Parker explained, there had never been a detailed plan to deal with major disasters affecting the city of Brisbane and the adjoining Redlands Shire. That might have been true, but it seemed to me that there were quite a few long-serving officers at the operations centre who would have a far better idea about how to formulate the sort of plans that Parker wanted. My whole career had been spent in operational policing. I had no experience of the kind of strategic task Parker was assigning me to. It didn't help that I would be working closely with his second-in-charge, Buckley.

***

Among other things, I had to devise mock exercises involving a hypothetical disaster striking the city. Members of different government departments would study the exercises and we'd have monthly counter-disaster meetings in which they outlined their plans to respond to the disaster.

I discovered that I enjoyed the work. It was a whole new direction in my policing career and I relished the challenge.

(It was ironic, I suppose, that Parker should have assigned me the task of writing counter-disaster plans, given that he would soon find himself at the centre of the biggest disaster ever to strike the Queensland Police Force.)

From my point of view, the job was going well. Mentally, I felt much better. Parker was still my boss but we had relatively little to do with each other. The Police Operations Centre was hardly the hotbed of corruption the Licensing Branch had been.

I had always made a point of keeping myself physically fit in order to cope with the demands of operational policing. I worked out at the gym and ran five or six days a week. I also had regular medical check-ups. When I visited my GP for another check-up I had no idea what was in store for me.

'How do you feel?' he asked me after taking my blood pressure.

'Great,' I said. 'Jumping out of my skin.'

He didn't say anything for a few moments.

'Is there a problem?' I asked.

He said, 'Your blood pressure is the second highest I have ever registered in a patient.'

My GP was around my age, early forties. During the time he had been practising medicine, I guessed he must have taken a few blood pressure readings. I asked, 'What happened to the patient whose reading was higher than mine?'

'I called an ambulance to the surgery and had her admitted to hospital—and that's exactly what I'm going to do with you.'

My first response was to panic. I was due to fly to Victoria in a couple of days to attend a course at the Counter Disaster College in Mount Macedon, where I would be working with local government staff, city and town planners, civil engineers, paramedics, fire fighters and civil aviation staff from all over Australia. I had never been to Victoria before and was desperate not to miss the course.

Foolishly, I begged him not to send me to hospital. If he let me go on the course, I said, I would take some leave and have a thorough rest. Working under Parker was not what I had wanted or expected when I moved to the operations centre, but in the circumstances I believed I was coping all right. Against his better judgement, I think, my GP let me talk him out of calling an ambulance.

A couple of days later I arrived at Mount Macedon, roughly 60 kilometres north-west of Melbourne. The township lies part-way up the mountain of the same name. The huge grey gums still bore the charcoal scars of the Ash Wednesday fires that tore through the area on 16 February 1983.

Forgetting—or ignoring—the strict advice of my GP to avoid hard physical exertion, I kept up my routine of daily road runs during the week I spent in Mount Macedon. I thought I understood my body better than he did, but I was wrong.

Returning to Brisbane, I was pleased to find that I was back on shift work. There was another surprise waiting for me:

THE BLACK CAT

Parker had been quickly promoted out of the Police Operations Centre and was now Assistant Commissioner for Crime and Services. He was now the third-highest ranking officer in the Queensland Police Force and had more power than ever. His meteoric rise through the ranks had already led to speculation that Parker was being groomed for the job of Commissioner. I'm sure I wasn't the only one thinking, 'Heaven forbid.'

***

Wednesday, 28 January 1987 was a blistering hot summer's day—hot enough to melt the bitumen on city streets. I was rostered on a 2 p.m. to 10 p.m. shift. In spite of the heat I decided to go for my daily workout at the gym before going to the office.

It was so hot inside the gym that I decided to cut my workout short, take a shower and go home for a nap before starting my shift. The morning classes were over and I had the gym to myself. I didn't feel the best. I remember thinking that if I collapsed in the shower I might not be discovered until late afternoon when office workers on their way home came to the gym to do their workouts.

As I was leaving the gym I stopped at reception to hand in my locker key. The manager, Veronica, took one look at me and said, 'Col, are you all right? You don't look too well.'

I was finding it difficult to breathe but I told myself I was only suffering heat exhaustion. Veronica called to her husband, John, who made me sit down. He asked me whether I needed a doctor but I said I was OK, it was only the heat. I walked out to my car, which had been in the sun all morning, but as soon as I sat inside I started to feel faint. I turned on the air-conditioning and began to feel a little better—at least well enough to drive the 2 kilometres to my home. But as I approached my house something told me to keep driving to the hospital. My breathing was returning to normal and I still refused to believe there was anything seriously wrong. It was only when my vision started to blur and I hit the kerb outside the hospital entrance that I knew I was in big trouble. Somehow I managed to park my car and start walking up the hill towards the main entrance. By now I was sweating profusely and seeing double. I staggered to the reception desk. When the receptionist asked me which doctor I had come to see, I said, 'Just get me any doctor.' The next thing I knew I was in a cubicle and people were doing tests on me. I could see a clock on the wall and mumbled to one of the nurses, 'How long before I can go? I have to start work at two o'clock.'

'You're not going to work,' he said. 'You're going straight into intensive care.'

I was having a heart attack and had only just made it to hospital. If I had gone home from the gym to have a sleep, as I intended, I would probably never have woken up.

No doubt there were some in the Queensland Police Force who would come to wish I hadn't.

NINE

Lifting the lid

On the evening of Monday, 11 May 1987, the day after my forty-third birthday, the ABC broadcast a *Four Corners* report called 'The Moonlight State'. By then I was back at work after my heart attack. The next morning I happened to meet Allen Bulger in the city. His face was ashen. He said, 'Did you watch *Four Corners* last night?' I replied facetiously, 'Yes, I thought they did a pretty good job.'

Bulger said, 'That bastard Powell, he's a bloody dog.' Nigel Powell, a former police officer, had supplied information to *Four Corners* and to the *Courier Mail* journalist Phil Dickie about corruption in the Licensing Branch. 'My bet is it won't amount to much anyway. It will blow over in a couple of days.'

'I guess we'll find out,' I said.

I returned just as Graeme Parker, now Assistant Commissioner for Crime and Services, arrived at headquarters. TV reporters and cameramen surrounded his car, jostling to get close enough with their hand-held microphones. For a while I stood there watching, confident that Parker would be far too preoccupied with the media frenzy to take any notice of me. I was close enough to hear one reporter say, 'Mr Parker, there have been some serious allegations made against you to the effect that you're corrupt. What have you to say in response?'

Before scurrying to the front door, Parker told the reporters that he was 'absolutely flabbergasted' by the allegations and had already instructed his solicitor to start defamation action.

Still smarting from the ignominious failure of his campaign to become prime minister, the Queensland premier, Joh Bjelke-Petersen, tried to stare down calls for an inquiry. But within twenty-four hours of the *Four Corners* program going to air, the Police Minister and Acting Premier, Bill Gunn, had announced what would become the Fitzgerald Commission of Inquiry. 'A series of police ministers have had these types of allegations hanging over their heads,' he said. 'They are not going to hang over mine.'

I doubt I was alone in thinking that the inquiry would be brief and ineffectual and primarily a device to ease the political pressure on the government.

My great fear was that the inquiry would turn into a re-run of the 1963 National Hotel Royal Commission, which investigated allegations that police were taking kickbacks from prostitution at Brisbane's National Hotel. The police supposedly involved in the racket denied everything. Witnesses were said to have been intimidated and threatened. Many Queenslanders considered the royal commission to have been a whitewash. Two decades later, the police were still taking kickbacks from prostitution.

The Fitzgerald Inquiry was not given the status of a royal commission but appointed by Order in Council. The initial terms of reference, prepared by the Justice department

LIFTING THE LID

and published in the Queensland *Government Gazette* on 26 May 1987, were mainly limited to matters arising out of the *Four Corners* investigation.

On 27 July 1987 the inquiry got under way with Police Commissioner Sir Terence Lewis as its first witness.

It was still six months since my heart attack but my health was still not the best. In mid-August I was admitted to the Prince Charles Hospital in Chermside for coronary surgery. I returned to work at the Police Operations Centre on 24 August. Four days later I was at home when the phone rang. The caller was a colleague who had been sitting in at the inquiry. 'Make sure you watch the news tonight,' he said. 'It will be on all channels. Harry Burgess has rolled over and it sounds like there are more to come.'

I was elated. I remembered what Parker had told reporters the day after the *Four Corners* program was aired about being 'flabbergasted'. I wondered what would be going through his mind now that his trusted offsider Harry Burgess had rolled over.

Word rapidly filtered through headquarters that Parker had left his office that afternoon, taking only personal items with him. The police departmental car allocated to him for official and private use was found in its parking bay beneath headquarters and the ignition keys had been left on his desk. Parker had obviously done a runner. I felt sorry for his personal assistant, a sergeant who was left to deal not only with the media baying for an interview but also with senior police from around the country who were far from happy about the suspicious disappearance of the Queensland Police Force's representative on the National Crime Authority.

Burgess's evidence sent a shock through the whole force. Nobody wanted to miss a word of what was being said at the inquiry. After Parker's vanishing act, Buckley instructed me to attend the inquiry every day and report back to him. He told me to take note of anything concerning Parker, which made me suspect that he knew where Parker was and that the two of them were still in touch.

It was a vital opportunity I couldn't let pass, so I asked Buckley, 'By the way, how is Mr Parker?' I caught him right off guard. He hesitated and stammered a reply. 'He's not too well at the moment.' I thought to myself, I bloody well bet he's not.

Buckley's request that I report back to him any mention of Parker confirmed to me that he wasn't aware of the very strained relationship between us. If Buckley had known what Parker thought of me, he would never have made the mistake of sending me to be his observer at the inquiry.

***

Since Bill Gunn's announcement of the Commission of Inquiry, not a day had passed when I hadn't thought about fronting up and telling everything I knew about corruption in the Licensing Branch. Two things held me back: apprehensiveness that the Fitzgerald Inquiry might turn out to be another whitewash, like the National Hotel Royal Commission; and fear for the safety of my family. Breaking the police code of silence would put not just me but my wife and children in danger. Would we be given full protection by the Commission of Inquiry? Would it end my career in the police and, if so, would we have to sell up and move to another state or territory or even leave the country? I was often paralysed with fear about how I would support my family and educate my children. How would they feel if they had to leave their school, their friends and our extended family?

Harry Burgess's decision to come clean must have given him some relief. It also bought him a full indemnity in return for telling everything he knew. Having worked in correctional centres in Western Australia and Queensland since my retirement from the police, I know that prison is a bad place for corrupt police. While they may be segregated from other prisoners for some of the time, they are rarely segregated at meal times. By rolling over, Burgess had spared himself the dangers of a prison sentence. But my motive for speaking out was not the same as Burgess's. I hadn't been taking money from brothel-owners and SP bookies. What I needed wasn't indemnity from prosecution but protection for myself and my family.

Burgess must have done a lot of thinking over the weekend. On Monday he was back in courtroom 29, where he confessed to corruptly receiving around $27,000 in bribes from Parker and others at the Licensing Branch. He also admitted to getting 'freebies' from prostitutes he was supposed to be protecting.

After two days in the witness box, Burgess stepped down to make way for a parlour madam who testified under the name Katherine James. I had met James soon after starting at the Licensing Branch. She was an attractive woman with long blonde hair and she reminded me of Olivia Newton-John, although spectators in the public gallery wouldn't have known because she was allowed to give evidence from behind a wooden screen. James had quite a history as a heroin user. She owned and operated a parlour with a name that might have been inspired by one of Olivia's films—Xanadu. It was on Stanley Street, Mater Hill, just south of the city of Brisbane. There was a bus stop right outside the parlour where students from St Laurence's College, a private Catholic school for boys, would gather each afternoon to catch the bus.

I remember naively asking Gary, my most trusted colleague, how such a good-looking woman could become involved in prostitution. 'Drugs, Col,' was Gary's reply. 'The money's good, it's cash in hand and that's what they need in order to support their habit.'

Parker and Bulger repeatedly instructed me to raid James's parlour. They said they wanted it closed down because it was too close to where schoolkids hung around waiting for the bus. Compared with most of the parlours I policed, Xanadu was opulent. It called itself a health club. There was a large reception area with three working rooms and showers. An area out the back was being prepared for spas. I think there was also space set aside for a gym. James had spent a lot of money setting up the business and Xanadu was providing fierce competition for nearby parlours run by Tilley and Hapeta. It was this, not the risk of corrupting schoolboys, that concerned Parker and Bulger.

When visiting the parlours for inspection or to make an arrest, I always insisted that my officers conducted themselves in a professional manner. After Gary informed me that a couple of the parlour madams had criminal records for using and supplying drugs, I began to make random checks, always with another officer present, to examine the girls for needle marks on their arms and feet. When they realised I was there to do my duty, and not to demand favours, some of the girls began to confide in me. Over time they became a valuable source of information.

I soon heard that Katherine James was falling behind in the payments she was making to corrupt police. I also found out that she was being pressured to supply sexual favours to one particular detective sergeant as well as to his sidekick, a detective senior constable. Both men were in the habit of visiting the premises alone after hours, in contravention of proper policing procedures and of the Licensing Branch's own policy guidelines. My information was that these corrupt police would stand over James for money on top of the bribes she was already paying to Parker and company.

Parker himself gave me instructions to have Xanadu's phones cut off. Then some of the girls were breached and summonsed. It was obvious that the next step was going to be to close it down. We were visiting the place virtually every day and James asked me why we were paying so much attention to Xanadu when there were other parlours nearby that were hardly touched. I told her—because this was my honest belief at the time—that we intended to shut her down because the parlour was next to a bus stop used by schoolkids. When I told her this, she just laughed. It was only a matter of days later that Xanadu closed.

Katherine James's evidence under oath really lifted the lid on police corruption. She wasn't scared to name the officers she knew to be corrupt. As a result of James's testimony Detective Sergeant John 'Bluey' O'Gorman, in his official capacity as president of the Queensland Police Union of Employees, began to attend the inquiry on a daily basis to monitor the evidence, because it implicated his members. Bluey was present throughout James's evidence and her cross-examination by counsel assisting the inquiry. It was Bluey who told me that when Katherine James was asked about me she replied that 'Sergeant Dillon was the only one from the Licensing Branch I found to be professional in his duties and never at any time did I consider him or those working under his control to be out of line'.

Not all the parlour madams were as truthful in their evidence to the inquiry. Ann Marie Tilley, for example, slandered the reputation of several police officers who I believe were innocent. When counsel assisting the inquiry asked Tilley whether I had ever demanded free liquor or sexual favours from the girls who worked in her parlours, she replied, 'I'm not too sure. I think he may have.' As a result of her accusation I was served with a notice of allegation by the inquiry. Of course Tilley could not offer any proof of this. I sometimes wondered whether Tilley's malice towards me went back to the day I interviewed her and Hector Hapeta at their house in Spring Hill. I now knew that the unwanted bottle of Chivas Regal whisky I had found in my locker had been a present from Tilley, delivered for her by Harry

Burgess. Was the false accusation she had made against me payback for not doing her bidding?

Katherine James spent nearly seven days in the witness box, sticking to her story in the face of fierce cross-examination by lawyers representing the police. The following Monday Commissioner Fitzgerald made his appeal for honest officers to come forward with information.

***

It was now or never, I told myself. That night I went to see my old friend Keith Harris. If anyone could give me advice, he could. 'Come on, Col,' he said. 'You're worried about something. Get it off your chest.'

I told Keith that I had decided to go to the inquiry. We sat in his downstairs hideaway, where Keith made his home brew, and talked the matter over. Like every policeman in Queensland, Keith knew the culture of the police force and understood its unwritten laws. When I told him that I was going to name the corrupt officers I had worked with at the Licensing Branch, he was very concerned. 'You're taking a big risk, Col,' he said. 'I hope you've thought about this.'

I said I had thought about little else for months.

It wasn't Parker and Burgess he was worried about but the shadowy figures in the background. In particular, he warned me about Tony Murphy, a detective who had been adversely named at the National Hotel Royal Commission. Murphy had a reputation for violence and was known as an enforcer for Frank Bischof, the corrupt former boss of the CIB. Shirley Brifman, a prostitute who accused Murphy of collecting bribes, had years ago been found dead under suspicious circumstances. Keith said, 'Murphy is quite capable of having you fixed up and if he had to, he'd do it himself.'

I knew Murphy's reputation but I also knew that I wouldn't be able to live with myself if I didn't tell the inquiry what I knew.

LIFTING THE LID

Before I left the house Keith took both my hands and squeezed them tightly. 'Take care, Marshall,' he said, using the nickname he had always called me by. 'I am very proud of you for the stand you're taking.' Then he added, more ominously, 'I hope the bastards look after you when this is all over.'

TEN

Fronting the Fitzgerald Inquiry

Courtroom 29 had been completely remodelled to accommodate the Fitzgerald Inquiry. The jury box and most of the public seating had been stripped out to make room for rows of extra tables for the lawyers. Reporters sat shoulder to shoulder with spectators in what was left of the public gallery.

Mr Ralph Devlin, junior counsel assisting, began by asking some general questions about the structure of the Licensing Branch and how it was divided into different squads: liquor, prostitution, pornography, racing and betting. He then asked me about the four-hundred dollar a month bribe I had been offered by Harry Burgess. Burgess had already come forward to the commission and admitted his corruption. Devlin now had Parker in his sights. I said Burgess's offer of a bribe had put me in a real quandary. My instincts told me that Burgess would not have been running a one-man show and that there would have been a round-table conference about making an approach to me.

Devlin asked me whether Burgess had warned me about not going to 'the boss' and I said he had.

> 'The term "the boss"—did you know then or did you come to know whom he meant when he referred to "the boss"?'
>
> 'Yes, I knew that he was referring to Inspector Parker as whenever I heard him speak to Inspector Parker he always referred to him as "boss".'
>
> 'Did he use his name, however, during this approach to you?'
>
> 'No.'
>
> 'Up until the time of the approach, had you heard anything in talk in the office to suggest that other persons were in receipt of money from somewhere, along the same lines as had been suggested to you?'
>
> 'No, sir. Not a thing.'
>
> 'Did you consider approaching Inspector Parker, nevertheless, to tell him of the approach?'
>
> 'No, I didn't . . . I considered it best not to.'
>
> 'Did you consider approaching persons of higher rank to acquaint them with the approach?'
>
> 'Yes, I did, but I just couldn't bring myself to take the risk.'

The next thing Mr Devlin wanted to ask me about was the bottle of whisky Burgess slipped into my locker shortly after I had knocked back his offer of a bribe.

> 'What occurred?'
>
> 'It was at Christmas time. I came to work one morning and I had occasion to go to my locker, which was locked, and to which I had the key—the only key. My locker

contained my service revolver, ammunition and other important departmental documentation. I opened my locker and I found a bottle of Scotch inside; a bottle of Chivas Regal. That completely floored me; to think that anyone could gain access to my locker. I didn't say anything to anybody. I waited, and it may have been, perhaps, the next day, or two days at the most, when I was next on duty when Harry Burgess approached me and said, "Did you get your Christmas pressie?" I replied, "I beg your pardon?" He said, "Did you get your present? There's a bottle of Scotch in your locker, and it's good stuff too." I replied, "Thanks." I didn't discuss it with him any further.'

'Did you inquire as to its origins?'

'Yes, I did.'

'What did you ask him about that?'

'I said, "Well, where is it from? Who is it from?" which I was anxious about. I wanted to know where it had come from or who had sent it to me. He just replied, "Look, don't worry about it. It's a present."'

'Well, how did you deal with that? What did you decide to do about that?'

'Again, not wanting to upset him or to cause any bad blood between he and I or, more importantly, not to let him think I posed a threat to him . . . I just took the Scotch and kept it in my possession.'

'Did you ever consume it?'

'Never.'

'Have a look at this, please. Did you produce that bottle to the Commission from your home?'

'Yes, sir, I did.'

'Has it ever been opened?'

'It still has its original seal on it.'
'It is a bottle of Chivas Regal Royal Salute?'
'That is correct.'
'Is that the bottle you received?'
'Yes, it is.'
'I tender that.'
'I used to speak to that bottle every night and say, 'Why did I ever bring you home?"'

That bottle of Chivas Regal, tendered as Exhibit 194, was the first concrete evidence of bribery inside the Licensing Branch to be given to the Commission of Inquiry.

Sometimes I had the feeling that Mr Devlin was leading me round in circles, but gradually I understood what he was trying to do. He was using me to paint a picture of the police force: only a few officers were actually corrupt, in the sense of taking bribes, but the system was such that it was dangerous for an honest police officer to speak out. You never knew who was talking to whom. If you told what you knew to a senior officer whom you knew to be honest, he might let something slip to another officer who was bent, and the personal repercussions could be very serious.

I was asked a lot of questions about drugs. There was not the slightest doubt in my mind, I told Devlin, that drugs were being moved through massage parlours operated by Hapeta and Tilley. There was a girl called Helen who, whenever I saw her, seemed to be off her face on drugs. The receptionist told me that they would find used syringes and needle heads, and while they could never catch her injecting herself, they were certain that the used syringes belonged to her. But whenever I made inquiries among the fellows I worked with, some of whom had been in the branch far longer than I had, they would say, 'It's got me beat. They know the policy. If they are caught with drugs, it's instant dismissal by the owners.' That might have been the policy, but they could see as well as I could that drugs were coming into the parlours.

I gave the inquiry the pages I had photocopied from the black accounts book I suspected of belonging to John the Jeweller, which contained entries such as 'Money paid to J.M. [John McKinnon aka John the Jeweller] via Lisa, $246 for loose diamonds; $167.33 commission from Carla' and so on. Some of the entries went as high as $1400 or $1500. I didn't believe for a second that these girls were really buying loose diamonds; they were buying heroin. When Mr Devlin asked me why I was so sure they were not spending money on jewellery, I answered:

> Because in my time when I moved through the massage parlours I took careful note in a caring sense. They were a section of our society which I really felt for, simply because I knew they were being used and abused . . . I had occasion to go to certain places where they lived and looked in their fridges, and I can tell you some of them could not even make themselves a Vegemite sandwich . . . their mode of dressing left a lot to be desired and from that I knew that they could not afford to buy pieces of jewellery that would be in any way consistent with some of the figures mentioned on those sheets, for by the time they paid their dues to the operators in the parlours and paid their fines there was very little left for them to spend on themselves, least of all on jewellery.

Proving that Parker and his cronies were receiving bribes was harder than it looked. While I was certain that they were on the take, I had never actually seen money change hands. The proof, as far as I was concerned, was in the way the Licensing Branch prosecuted some while leaving others alone. Katherine James had already given evidence to the commission about how her parlour, Xanadu, was closed down but not those belonging to Hapeta and Tilley. The same thing was true with unlicensed clubs. Mr Devlin asked me whether it was true that Geraldo Bellino's World by Night strip club operated continuously without a licence.

'Always.'

'Pharaoh's appeared to operating in a similar way?'

'Yes.'

'Did you ever have contact with the unlicensed club Hollywood's during your time?'

'Yes, I may have gone there once.'

'And it appeared to be operating on a nightly basis, again without a licence?'

'Yes, on a par with Lennons or any of your leading hotels.'

'Did it cross your mind to inquire as to why these places were just continuing on a nightly basis?'

'No. I accepted the fact that the procedures or policies in respect to those establishments must have been ... well in existence prior to my arrival and that one was expected to just go along and do what one was told.'

'Do you ever recall an instruction from above you to close one of those places down once and for all?'

'I'm sorry, which places?'

'World by Night, Pharaoh's or Hollywood's?'

'No, never.'

'There were other places, however, which were the subject of concentrated action by you which resulted in them ceasing to trade or apparently ceasing to trade in liquor?'

'Yes.'

One of these was a restaurant close to the Breakfast Creek Hotel. I was given instructions to go there and, by using an agent, to obtain evidence of the unlawful sale of liquor. The owner, Cono Scafidi, more or less asked me to explain why he was receiving raid after raid when other unlicensed premises such as World by Night, Hollywood's and others in the city were allowed to ply their trade in unlawful liquor unhindered. I remember feeling embarrassed at being unable to give him an answer. The answer I ought to have given him was, 'Because they are paying Parker for protection and you are not.'

After Mr Devlin had led me through my evidence I braced myself for the cross-examination. There were barristers wall to wall representing so-called 'interested parties' and I could feel them itching to have a go at me.

Leon Taeffe, who was representing the police unions, wanted to know exactly when I had made up my mind to disclose Harry Burgess's effort to bribe me: was it before Harry admitted to being corrupt or after?

> 'What I am asking you is when it was you first told the Commission's officers about that attempted bribe—you only told them recently, did you not?'
>
> 'That's correct, yes.'
>
> 'I am just trying to establish whether you told them that after Burgess had given evidence here or before he had given evidence here.'
>
> 'I think it would be after.'

Others asked me the same question. I felt they were trying to suggest that if Burgess hadn't come forward and admitted his corruption, I wouldn't have come forward myself—that if Burgess hadn't mentioned it first, I would have kept my mouth shut. If they were implying that I was scared, they were right—I knew what had happened to the witnesses at the National Hotel Royal Commission and I wanted to make bloody sure it wasn't going to happen to me. After Burgess rolled over, I knew the game was up for the rest of them.

Leon Taeffe was a good man. He knew I wasn't well. Every now and then he would mouth the words, 'Are you okay?' to which I would nod my head.

In the gallery, people were riveted to their seats as a succession of barristers tried to pick holes in my evidence. My two days on the stand were gruelling. At one point my elbow slipped off the rail and I almost fell onto the floor. Leon jumped out of his seat and looked up at Mr Fitzgerald, who said he had been advised about the state of my health and was trying not to prolong my stay in the witness box.

My cross-examination finished before lunch on Thursday, 17 September. Before I stepped down, Leon Taeffe asked me whether there had been any response from fellow police officers to the evidence I had given. I answered that many had been in touch to offer their support.

'Have you received any criticism?'

'None at all, none at all.'

'You are obviously proud to be a police officer, is that so?'

'I formed the intention of being a police officer at the age of four years and I never ever deviated; I went straight down the line to being just that.'

'You have come along here to give the Inquiry what assistance you can?'

'Yes, sir.'

'Do you have any message for any other police officers who may have information that may assist?'

'I sure have, and it is this: I would like them to now, at this point of time in our policing history, to stand up, boldly step forward and speak out about what they know of any crime or corruption within this State that is presently eroding, and that has for a great number of years eroded, our great police force like a cancerous growth. Step up and be counted. Do your part in helping to remove this cancer so that we can get on the road to restoring the good image that we once had, and that we can restore the faith in the public that we serve, and I ask, I implore, all members of the public, the decent members of the public, please do not write us off. We are there. The greater percentage of us are honest. We strive, we fight courageously to serve you, to care for you, to keep the streets clean, so that you and your family can walk the streets, not frightened, not to be harassed, and if you support us, if you give us the support we need, you will be rewarded by a great body of men and women who you will find will not hold back but will be out there straining to the limits to give you the best police service that I feel you so richly deserve.'

As I thanked Mr Taeffe for giving me the opportunity to speak, the whole court including all those in the gallery stood up and started to clap. I didn't know what to think. I expected Mr Fitzgerald to put an immediate stop to it. But instead he said, 'I certainly would not stop the applause. I think everybody is very impressed with your evidence, Sergeant. I cannot indicate to you any view about its credibility, of course, because I have to listen to a whole lot of other people during the course of this.'

Outside, the media were waiting for me. TV crews surged across the courtyard and newspaper reporters converged on me from all directions. I couldn't believe that the evidence I had just given would create the media interest that it did. More journalists were waiting on the front steps of Police Headquarters. They swarmed towards me, clamouring for interviews. After two days in the witness box I was utterly exhausted. I could hardly say a word and had to be rescued by staff from the police media unit.

While I was heartened by the positive reaction from both the media and the general public, I knew that I would not get the same reception from all my colleagues. So far, as I told the Commission of Inquiry, the comments had all been favourable, but I knew that wouldn't last.

***

I wasn't the only witness to give evidence to the Commission of Inquiry on 17 September. Before adjourning for lunch, Commissioner Fitzgerald made a surprise announcement:

> An important witness cannot attend the Commission for what I am advised is a genuine reason nor can a public hearing take place elsewhere since for security reasons the witness's whereabouts must remain unknown. I regret it if that sounds melodramatic. I propose to go to that witness to enable short important evidence to be given. No other person will be named in that evidence at this point and there will be no need for any person appearing before the Commission to be present or represented. The witness will be legally represented. I will then return and the evidence will be read out together with the witness's name at public sittings of the Commission this afternoon. The witness will, in due course, be called to give evidence and be available for cross-examination at a public sitting. The only secret matter will be the witness's whereabouts and, until later today, the name of the witness, and the content of the brief evidence to be given this morning. Both will be publicly disclosed later today. I direct that no attempt be made to follow me or to discover the witness's whereabouts.

FRONTING THE FITZGERALD INQUIRY

The unnamed witness was Parker, who was apparently too ill to get out of bed. When Fitzgerald said 'for security reasons the witness's whereabouts must remain unknown' I couldn't help thinking of my own situation. Nobody said anything about keeping my whereabouts unknown. My face was all over the newspapers and my address and telephone number were in the phone book.

Parker's bedside hearing lasted only a few minutes. Gary Crooke QC, senior counsel assisting, reported what had been said:

'Could we have your full name?'

'Graeme Robert Joseph Parker.'

'Your former rank in the police force?'

'Assistant Commissioner (Crime and Services).'

'Yesterday evening did you resign from the police force?'

'Yes, I did.'

'Is it the case that you have admitted to the Commission that you were involved in corruption as a police officer?'

'Yes.'

'Have you also, Mr Parker, provided information to the Commission including information involving other police officers in corruption?'

'Yes.'

Parker had served with the likes of Frank Bischof, Tony Murphy and Glen Hallahan and was a survivor of the National Hotel Royal Commission. I had worked under him both at the Licensing Branch and in the 1960s at Innisfail and knew he had been on the take for two decades. He understood the dark arts of fabricating evidence and I was astounded to hear that he had not only admitted to corruption himself but had agreed to roll on others.

***

Because Linda had gone away with the children, I went home that day to an empty house. My phone was ringing hot with calls from the media. In the end I had to leave it off the hook so that I could get some peace. My appearance at the commission was the lead story on several of the TV news bulletins. The ABC gave the most detailed coverage, using actors to re-enact the events.

My home was on a busy arterial road and I started noticing cars slowing down as they passed. A couple stopped in front of my place. People were shining torches through my windows. I had no idea whether they were reporters after an interview or other people with more sinister motives. At no time had Devlin or anyone else from the Commission of Inquiry suggested that my family and I might need some form of witness protection. I felt totally alone.

After the evening news had finished I heard my front door bell chime. I had all the lights turned off but for one in a back room which could not be seen from the road. There was a car in my driveway which I immediately recognised as belonging to my old mate Keith Harris. I opened the front door and saw Keith and his wife, Ronnie. Keith embraced me. He was very emotional. 'Col,' he mumbled, 'I said to Ronnie today, "What have I done to him? I've thrown him to the wolves."'

'No, Keith,' I said, 'You didn't throw me to the wolves. Going to the commission was my decision. You warned me what the consequences could be. I just wish I had thought more about my family. There's going to be payback for sure.'

'Don't worry about those bastards,' said Keith. 'You did the right thing and Ronnie and I are proud of you. There's plenty of honest blokes who could have done what you did but they didn't have the courage. You can hold your head up high.'

I appreciated his support but holding my head up high wasn't going to do me much good when I walked into Police Headquarters the next day as the man who'd ratted on his mates.

Around nine o'clock the phone rang. I put the phone to my ear but before I could open my mouth I heard Linda screaming at me. 'What the bloody hell have you done, Col? Your face is all over the TV. What's going to happen to us? You told me you wouldn't be dobbing on anyone and that's exactly what you've done. We'll have to pull the kids out of school. They won't be safe anymore. None of us will be.'

I tried to calm her down. I said we would be looked after; the Commission of Inquiry would make sure that nothing happened to us.

'Are you sure of that?' she asked.

'Of course I'm sure,' I told Linda. 'We'll have protection. The police won't let us down.'

Naively, I still believed the Queensland Police Force was on my side. In truth it was my enemy, but I didn't know it.

ELEVEN

Doing things as they should be done

I was due to return to my job the next day. I had a sleepless night wondering how things would be in the morning when I walked into the office. Would I get the cold shoulder, or worse? I was especially apprehensive about Buckley's reaction. For the last two weeks I had been giving him daily reports on goings-on at the inquiry. I could only imagine the look on his face when he found out that the witness who had just come forward with concrete evidence of corruption in the Licensing Branch was me. I had no doubt that Buckley had known where Parker was hiding and that the pair had been in contact, which would be awkward for him now that Parker had rolled over. Had my evidence been the last straw that forced Parker to admit his corruption? If so, then I could safely add Buckley to the list of police with a grudge against me.

I caught the train to Roma Street Station as I always did. The train was packed and everybody seemed to have their head in a newspaper. The first few pages were dominated by the Fitzgerald Inquiry. There were pictures of me in full uniform. As I stood there, people started recognising me. Complete strangers reached out and shook my hand, saying, 'Good on you, Sergeant.'

A lady grabbed my hand and said, 'Thank you for what you've done for the police force and the people of Queensland.'

As I got off at Roma Street a man dressed in tradesman's clothes approached me and without speaking pressed an envelope into my hand before he disappeared into the crowd. On the short walk from the station to headquarters, more people congratulated me. Motorists and taxi drivers started blowing their car horns and waving at me. Overnight I had become a public figure. I appreciated the support but at the same time it made me nervous. I felt as though I had nowhere to hide.

I had only just sat down at my desk when Superintendent Frank O'Gorman came by. At that time he was working in the office of the commissioner. There was no reason for him to come to see me but he told me he wanted to express his personal gratitude for my attending the inquiry and giving evidence. He also took the opportunity to address all my colleagues and gave a short speech that left no one in any doubt that he supported my actions.

Frank and I then moved to somewhere more private, where he again shook my hand and gave me a piece of paper with his home address and private telephone number on it. 'Col,' he said, 'I really hope you don't cop any flak over the stand you've taken, but if you do, don't hesitate to call me any time, day or night.' I want to put it on record that Frank O'Gorman was the only serving commissioned officer in the entire Queensland Police Force to make such an offer. Nobody else came close to matching Frank's promise of unconditional support. Sometime earlier I had lent Frank a book which he now returned to me. Inside was a handwritten note that read:

DOING THINGS AS THEY SHOULD BE DONE

Dear Col,

With my compliments and sincere thanks for your courage. 'You're a better man than I am Gunga Din.'

Regards,
Frank O'Gorman
18 September, 1987.

I then opened the envelope which the stranger had placed in my hand outside the railway station. It contained a card with a simple but heartwarming message: 'Thank you, Sergeant Dillon, for restoring my faith in the Queensland Police Force.'

I'm sorry to say that I never saw that man again to thank him for his kind words, which reassured me that I had done the right thing in speaking out. Without the support I received from the public I would have found it very hard to cope with the difficulties that lay ahead.

I could describe in two words the support I was given by the Queensland Police Force: Bugger All.

* * *

I had to wait some time for my first meeting with Buckley, since he had taken a week's leave beginning the day after I gave my evidence at the inquiry. I was due to give him a detailed briefing on the current status of the Counter Disaster Plan I had been working on with Tony Blacksell of the State Emergency Service.

While I waited for Buckley to return, the newspapers pestered me for interviews. I had never done a media interview before and was glad for the help I received from the police media unit. The dust hadn't settled from my appearance at the inquiry and I was deluged with mail from all around the country and even from New Zealand. The Fitzgerald Inquiry was now the biggest show in town.

Every morning there were long queues for the few seats in the public gallery. Spectators turned up with their cut lunches and thermos flasks so that they wouldn't have to leave the court precincts and risk losing their seats.

At work, the phone never stopped. I would get calls on other extensions, and when I went to take the call there would be no one there. These became too frequent for me to be able to dismiss them as missed calls or faulty connections. After a while I asked the switchboard to take the name of each caller; if the person wasn't prepared to give their name I refused to take the call. Calls to the 000 emergency lines were always recorded, but the calls I was getting always came in on the normal lines, which were not recorded. I knew that some of these had to be from fellow police.

A woman caller, who wouldn't give me her name, told me that she had information about serious police corruption which needed to be put before the inquiry. She refused to come in to Police Headquarters and suggested I meet her somewhere else. She had no fixed address, she said, but slept in the back of her car and moved around from place to place. She stressed that I was to come alone. I told her that unless she was prepared to meet on my terms then we wouldn't meet at all. I never heard from her again.

I was sure the mystery callers and silent callers were attempting to intimidate me and I knew the situation could only get worse. Quite a number of police had now been adversely named at the inquiry and some of these, I realised, would have liked nothing more than to have me set up.

After a few days I contacted Pat Nolan, who was representing all police on behalf of the police union. Pat advised me under no circumstances to go anywhere by myself or to meet anyone claiming to have information about corruption. When I told him about the call from the mystery women who lived in a car, Pat insisted on making a note of the details.

DOING THINGS AS THEY SHOULD BE DONE

Finally Buckley returned to work and I was able to brief him on my Counter Disaster Plan. Not a single word was said about my having given evidence at the inquiry. Buckley was a wily operator, quite a few years my senior in both age and service. He was a part of the old brigade and, to coin a phrase, he knew where the bodies were buried. He was also known to be well connected in the 'right' circles. I had heard from my own sources that Buckley was not travelling well, but nothing in his behaviour towards me showed it.

By now I had started to get phone calls at home. The callers never spoke but I could hear them breathing. The calls came either very late at night or in the early hours of the morning. People also started ringing a prominent businessman who had the same first name and surname as me. One day he contacted me to see if my family was OK. He wasn't worried for his own safety as his house had a very sophisticated alarm system. His advice was to ask the police to step up their patrols during the night and to keep a closer watch on my home. I didn't tell him that there were no patrols and that nobody was keeping watch on my home. As far as the Commission of Inquiry and the police were concerned, I could look after myself.

My evidence to the inquiry, combined with Burgess's admission of corruption and Parker's bedside confession, had shattered the reputation of the Queensland Police Force. The inquiry was gaining momentum by the day. Police morale had hit rock bottom. Operational police were doing their duty with little in the way of supervision or decisive leadership.

Limited indemnities had been offered by Fitzgerald as an inducement to corrupt police to roll over, but some were still holding out.

Tony Blacksell and I had completed our Counter Disaster Plans for Brisbane and the Redlands Shire and I had returned to shift work at the Police Operations Centre. Buckley was still in charge but our relationship had continued to deteriorate as a result of my giving evidence at the inquiry.

Buckley's ongoing contact with Parker at a time when Parker was wanted by the inquiry, and his failure to assist the inquiry by reporting Parker's whereabouts, had left him wide open to disciplinary action or worse. (A year later Bulger, Parker's second-in-charge at the Licensing Branch, was dismissed from the police after admitting that he had known the whereabouts of Jack Reginald Herbert when Herbert was being sought by the inquiry. Herbert became famous—or I should say infamous—as the 'bagman' who collected and distributed bribes at the Licensing Branch.)

Buckley and I were still avoiding each other when I received notification from the office of the commissioner that I was being seconded from the Police Operations Centre to the newly created Independent Task Force. I didn't know much about the task force but I knew there was no future for me at the operations centre working under Buckley's command.

***

The Independent Task Force was to run concurrently with and be supervised by the Commission of Inquiry. Its commander was Inspector John Huey, who had worked for a short time with me at the Police Operations Centre before moving to the Fraud Squad. A former detective who was always impeccably dressed and had a fondness for distinctive ties, Huey and I were not close but we chatted from time to time.

Huey told me that the task force would operate independently of the police and that our headquarters would be in the Brisbane CBD, close to the law courts where the Fitzgerald Inquiry was sitting. Huey was very particular about the kind of person he wanted—and didn't want—for the task force. He refused to have anyone from the Criminal Investigation Branch and said he planned to recruit all of our staff

DOING THINGS AS THEY SHOULD BE DONE

from the general duties uniform sector of the police force. His preference was for young officers with a strong desire to become detectives. He left it up to me to identify suitable candidates, but he made sure he conducted the interviews by himself.

Our brief was to investigate a sophisticated car-stealing racket that was said to involve corrupt police including detectives from the Auto Theft Squad.

At our first meeting Huey gave orders that we were not to fraternise with police outside the task force or to visit the police force social club. This, he insisted, was a small price to pay for belonging to an elite squad. In case any of us were not convinced, Huey announced that he had ways of finding out if anyone had disobeyed his instructions and that transgressors would be instantly dismissed. Many of the younger officers were aghast when they heard this. Simply by volunteering for the task force, they risked being ostracised by other police; now here was their commanding officer ordering them to have nothing to do with their friends and colleagues. It wasn't a good start.

Shortly afterwards I ran into a respected lawyer whom I had known for many years. He asked me what I was doing at the task force and mentioned another attached detective, who had a reputation as a fabricator of evidence. I had met this detective when I was a young constable at the Brisbane magistrates' court. He had come up to me while I was waiting to give evidence and said, 'Anytime you ever need any help with a case just come and see me and I'll show you what to do.' At the time I had been gratified by his offer of help, but afterwards I was warned by older and wiser police to stay away from him. Knowing this man's reputation, I worried about the pressures that would be put on the young officers I'd helped recruit to the task force.

The Commission of Inquiry was breaking new ground every day. The newspapers were filled with fresh allegations of corruption. Reports flowed into our office that car theft was prevalent across the state, but so far we hadn't found any evidence that police were involved. However, an investigation was under way that would soon have devastating consequences for me and my family.

***

On 17 March 1988 a young detective named Tyron 'Mango' Mangakahia had given a briefing at Police Headquarters. Mango was working undercover to infiltrate the drug trade. Representatives of the Drug Squad, the Auto Theft Squad and the Fraud Squad were invited. The purpose of the meeting was to develop a strategy to deal with serious crimes coming to light through the work of the Commission of Inquiry. Through an informant, Mango had heard of a serving police officer working for a career criminal at the centre of a large-scale stolen car racket.

Two months later I received a phone call from Mango stating that one of our major targets, 'Max', was preparing to flee the country. I told Huey and as a result we picked up Max and brought him in for questioning about his involvement in the stolen car racket. Max immediately offered to roll and to give us the names of corrupt police.

That afternoon my cousin Ivan, who was stationed at Broadbeach police station, phoned and left a message for me. I'd known Ivan all his life and used to nurse him as a baby; he was the only one of my family to follow me into the police force and as a result there was a close bond between us. When Ivan told me he was being transferred to the Gold Coast, I took him aside and gave him some fatherly advice about what he could expect as a policeman on the Gold Coast.

I warned him that there were certain police who had been working on the Gold Coast for a long time—too long— and that some were taking money from criminals. Ivan assured me that I had nothing to worry about and that he would never let me down or bring dishonour on our family. I believed him.

The net was closing around the police involved in the stolen car racket. The task force had identified a panel beating and repair shop business on the Gold Coast that was acting as a front for one of the major car-theft syndicates. This supposedly legitimate business acted as the receiving centre for stolen cars that were then rebirthed and sold, sometimes through used-car sale yards. We had information that a police officer working on the Gold Coast was involved in the racket. Due to his impressive physique, he was given the nickname 'Arnold Schwarzenegger'.

On the instructions of the Commission of Inquiry, a video camera was covertly installed inside the panel-beating workshop. Watching the surveillance tapes, we had no trouble identifying Arnold Schwarzenegger as he entered the workshop. The sight of him made me feel sick in my guts: it was my cousin Ivan. I immediately advised the other detectives in the room that I could positively identify who 'Schwarzenegger' was, but I did not say he was my cousin. I wanted to break it to Huey first.

After telling Huey that Schwarzenegger was my cousin Ivan, I asked to step down from the investigation, or at least from the Gold Coast aspect of it. Given the serious nature of the issue, I expected him to refer it straight to his boss at the Commission of Inquiry, Bob Needham, counsel assisting. Huey, however, said that as far as he was concerned there was no need for me to step down. (By now Huey was well aware that there was unrest in the task force and that a number of the younger members wanted to leave; a mass exodus would look bad for him and he had made it clear that I was staying.)

Our experts on auto theft had the tedious job of trawling through thousands of motor vehicle records for engine and chassis numbers. They could tell at a glance if an engine number didn't belong to a certain make and model of vehicle; the owners would then be visited by members of the task force who would examine the suspect vehicle. In the course of their searches, the specialists came across two motor vehicles registered to my cousin Ivan at two different addresses. (I knew that one of the addresses would be his father's at Moreton Bay.) One of the vehicles was a late-model 4WD whose engine number did not match its year and model. That was enough to justify the task force paying Ivan a visit.

When I returned Ivan's phone call he told me he had just phoned to see how I was doing. This was odd, as he had never phoned me before. Ivan knew I worked for the task force; I realised straight away that he was fishing for information about the stolen cars investigation. I didn't tell him anything. I felt hurt and angry but most of all I felt betrayed.

We now had enough to raid the panel-beating shop and arrest the principals behind the Gold Coast racket. On the night of the raid Ivan was working a night shift, midnight to 8 a.m. I travelled with Huey to the Broadbeach police station. Ivan and his partner were out on patrol so we had the duty officer call them back to the station.

A few minutes later Ivan walked into the station. The moment he saw me he dropped his head, realising that his career as an officer in the Queensland Police was over. He would also have known that if he was convicted he would be facing a gaol sentence.

I took no part in interviewing Ivan. Huey asked me to drive Ivan home to collect all the government property issued to him by the Queensland Police Force.

The two of us were alone in the car. We drove for some time in silence before Ivan grabbed my hand and squeezed it hard. He was a giant of a man but his voice was almost breaking. 'I'm sorry I let you down, Col,' he said.

(Left) Aged sixteen and studying first aid.
(Right) Constable First Class, aged twenty-five

Me and a friend. I'm seventeen years old and the world is ahead of me.

(Left) With my two children, Sandra and Anthony.
(Right) On the set of *Police State*, 1989.

Outside my barrister's chambers after giving evidence
to the Fitzgerald Inquiry, 17 September 1987.

An inspector in the Professional Standards Unit, 1991.

Just before my retirement.

With my mother, who gave me the ethical framework and resilience to stand up to corruption in the Queensland Police Force.

(Left) From my clippings folder. Receiving an honorary doctorate from Queensland University of Technology, 2000. (Right) With Linda and my grandson Jackson.

In happy retirement, with Mum and my three grandchildren, Jackson, Ashleigh and Magnolia.

DOING THINGS AS THEY SHOULD BE DONE

I said, 'Ivan, you know what you've done. They are going to send you to gaol. The only chance you've got is to tell us everything you know about this gang you're running with. There's no point covering for anyone and taking the full rap yourself. You don't owe those bastards anything.'

Ivan replied, 'Trust me, Col. I'll tell them everything. I'm not going to cover for anyone and I won't be fighting it when we go to court.'

After we returned to the Broadbeach police station, Ivan was formally arrested. He appeared later that morning in the Southport magistrates' court where he was committed to the District Court for sentence.

The next morning when I arrived at work, one of the more senior detectives approached me and said, 'Did you hear what the Guv [Huey] did with your cousin before he was arrested and charged?'

'No,' I said. 'Tell me.'

He said, 'After you told the Guv that Ivan had confessed and given up names, the Guv decided to question him again.' I didn't like the implication that maybe I had gone soft on Ivan because he was my cousin.

'Go on,' I said. 'What was Huey up to?'

He said, 'The Guv promised your cousin that if he came clean and told him everything, particularly about any other coppers who were involved, he would make sure his father wasn't charged with any offence because if he was, he would also end up in gaol.'

'What did my cousin say?' I asked.

'He told the Guv he'd already told us everything but the Guv kept pressuring him by saying it was up to Ivan whether or not his father went to gaol.'

I knew the police had gone to Moreton Bay and that Ivan's father had been arrested for being in possession of the 4WD, but telling Ivan his father was going to gaol was just bullshit. If Ivan's father had committed an offence I wanted to make sure he was charged. I wasn't going to let Ivan get mixed up in one of Huey's deals.

I went straight to Huey's office and stood in his doorway. Huey looked up at me and smiled. 'Col,' he said, 'what can I do for you?'

I said, 'I've just found out that you promised Ivan you wouldn't charge his father with any offences if Ivan gave up his mates in the car-stealing racket.'

'That's right,' Huey said.

'But I told you Ivan had already given us everything he knew.'

I could see Huey clenching his fists. He said, 'What are you trying to tell me, Col?'

I said, 'If you don't charge Ivan's father as he should be charged for receiving a stolen vehicle, I'll make sure you are looking at departmental charges.'

Huey was so angry he couldn't speak. He smashed his clenched fist on the desk. I stared at him for a few moments before walking away.

Some people might wonder why I was so keen to have one of my own relatives charged. My answer is, you either do things as they are supposed to be done or you don't. It didn't matter that Ivan and his father were members of my own family: if they had committed an offence I was going to make sure they were charged. In my book you can't be half honest: bending the rules is halfway towards making them up yourself. If it hadn't been for the likes of Frank Bischof and Tony Murphy and Graeme Parker making up the rules themselves, we wouldn't have needed the Commission of Inquiry.

TWELVE

An undercover officer's cover is blown

The commission hadn't finished with me. Towards the end of May 1988 I received a phone call from Ralph Devlin asking me to come in to discuss further evidence about the SP betting industry. The next morning as I stepped out of the lift on the second floor I found myself face to face with Harry Burgess. It was the first time I had seen Burgess since the bubble burst. I was shocked by his appearance. He looked to be a broken man, haggard and worn with drooping shoulders. 'Hello, Harry,' I said. 'How are you?'

Burgess gave me a cold stare and replied tersely, 'Life goes on.' The lift door closed and that was the last time that I ever saw him.

I was annoyed that Devlin had called me in knowing there was a strong possibility that Burgess and I might bump into each other. Such a meeting under the circumstances was hardly going to be pleasant. When I made it clear that

I wasn't impressed, Devlin replied facetiously, 'It makes life interesting, doesn't it?'

To him it seemed like a joke, but to me it was deadly serious. I was still receiving anonymous phone calls. Some of the callers said nothing but others were abusive and threatening. My guess was that most of these calls were from corrupt police still in the force or their mates and sympathisers. I had reported the fact that I was receiving threatening phone calls and my report had been ignored. It was one more thing that my family and I would just have to learn to live with.

One day I arrived for work to discover that one of my desk drawers was unlocked, though I always took care to leave them locked. There were no signs of forced entry. This particular drawer contained my service revolver and personal papers.

I mentioned the incident later to a colleague whom I trusted. He told me that he had gone to my desk looking for a set of car keys the day before and had found both my desk drawers locked. Obviously someone was playing games, but I couldn't help feeling that there was a sinister side to it. I remembered the bottle of Chivas Regal Harry Burgess had put in my locker when we worked together at the Licensing Branch. Was this a practical joke or a warning?

I told another sergeant what had happened. The sergeant told me with a grin it would be virtually impossible to open such a drawer without forcing it and then in the blink of an eye he opened it with me watching. I didn't consider it prudent to push the matter any further but from that day on I kept my firearm and other personal items somewhere safer.

* * *

The Independent Task Force had been set up to spearhead the investigation of corruption. I was in my office one afternoon when I received a telephone call from Detective Senior

AN UNDERCOVER OFFICER'S COVER IS BLOWN

Sergeant Alan Freeman of the Drug Squad. He wanted to know who had given the order to arrest a target (I'll call him 'Stan') and charge him with conspiracy to commit murder. Freeman, was pretty stirred up. He told me that Stan's arrest had blown the cover of our undercover agent, Mango, and exposed one of Mango's informants. According to Freeman, the Drug Squad had been running a major operation and was on the brink of infiltrating a big drug ring. As a result of Stan's arrest, the whole operation was going to have to be aborted.

The following evening I received a call from Mango. I had just sat down to watch the report of the Fitzgerald Inquiry on the evening news. Mango told me that he was calling from his informant's garage. He said that one of the targets of our car-stealing investigation had just turned up in a stolen vehicle. The target was high on drugs and had threatened the informant's parents for money. Mango asked me what he should do.

I said, 'Leave it with me and I'll refer it to Huey, and he'll do whatever's necessary'.

Gradually the pieces of the jigsaw were coming together. We had made some good arrests. One person alone had been charged with 304 counts of auto theft. We received information from a rollover that bribes were being paid to four detectives in the Auto Theft Squad of the Brisbane CIB.

Our investigations into the car-stealing racket extended beyond Queensland. In July Huey announced that we were sending two detectives to Perth to explore links to a Queensland syndicate.

Our workload continued to grow and in August the Commission of Inquiry told Huey to recruit another inspector and four more plain clothes officers. Within a month the Independent Task Force would be expanded to three task forces, designated A, B and C. Somehow, all three were going to be sharing the same cramped office space.

Then, out of the blue, I received another call from Mango. He had not been in contact since the incident in the garage. He sounded on edge. He told me he had been to a meeting that day with a pair of drug dealers and that he believed his cover had been blown. According to Mango, one of the dealers accused him straight out of being a 'narc' (US slang for a narcotics agent) and of having worn a wire to their previous meeting. He told Mango the information had come from someone in the task force. Mango denied everything, and did not respond when one of the dealers tried to catch him out by using the name 'Mango'.

In light of what he had told me I held grave fears for Mango's safety and begged him to 'come in', but he seemed to think he was safer where he was. Coming in had its own risks. Before hanging up, Mango warned me to watch my back in case the people who had sold him out did the same to me.

It turned out that my instincts about who had given up Mango were correct. The next day I got a telephone call from Mango's controller at the Drug Squad, who identified the person who had blown Mango's cover to the drug dealers. He said that the same person had told the dealers about Mango wearing a wire at one of their meetings. I wasn't surprised when he told me that Mango's undercover colleagues were livid at what had been done to Mango and were all for flogging this person for endangering Mango's life.

Morale at the task force continued to deteriorate. When Huey told me that I would have to vacate my office for the new inspector, I told him that it didn't bother me as I was due for promotion and would be moving on soon. 'No you won't, Col,' he said. 'You're here for the duration.'

The Commission of Inquiry had some big names in its sights and Huey wanted sergeants to carry out the investigations. The biggest name of all was that of the police commissioner, Sir Terence Lewis. Investigating Lewis, Huey made a point of telling everyone, 'will be my job'.

AN UNDERCOVER OFFICER'S COVER IS BLOWN

On 16 August 1988 Inspector Allen Bulger was sacked by Minister for Police and Acting Premier Bill Gunn, on charges of corruption. He was convicted of perjury and received the second-longest prison sentence after Terry Lewis—twelve years.

I couldn't help feeling a bit sorry for him. Bulger was a happy-go-lucky character. He was a heavy drinker and smoker and loved to bet on the racehorses, but he wasn't exactly a racehorse himself. The word indolent just about sums him up: he wouldn't work in an iron lung. Around the middle of September Huey came to me with one of his mysterious requests. My shift was due to end at 3 p.m. but Huey asked me to return to the office at 10 p.m. to get the interview rooms ready. The Commission of Inquiry, he said, was going to do a raid and the interviews would be done in our rooms. He told me they could turn up any time after 10 p.m. and once they had arrived I could go home. I knew better than to ask him who the target was, since I knew he wouldn't tell me.

At about 10.30 p.m. Brendan Butler, a solicitor with the Commission of Inquiry, arrived at our office and told me that he would wait there for his colleagues who were conducting a raid. Butler didn't seem in the mood to talk, at least not to me, so I sat at my desk doing some paperwork until about 1 a.m., when I heard voices in the reception area near the lifts.

At last Butler turned to me and said, 'Col, I suppose you're wondering what's going on here tonight?'

I said, 'I dare say I'll find out soon enough.'

I could hear someone giving directions to whoever was with them to walk straight ahead. The other person didn't reply but I could hear his wheezing and gasping as he approached my office. I didn't need to see him to know that the person they had in their custody was Hector Brandon Hapeta, the so-called vice king of Brisbane and the Gold Coast.

As two detectives ushered him towards one of the interview rooms, Hapeta looked into my office and mumbled, 'Goodnight, Col,' to which I replied, 'Goodbye, Hector.'

Hapeta was one of the principal targets of the Fitzgerald Inquiry and was named in its terms of reference. He had been arrested not for corruption but for trafficking in heroin, partly on the basis of evidence I had given the inquiry about the sale of drugs in the massage parlours. My strong belief, then and now, is that in going after Hapeta for trafficking drugs in the massage parlours the inquiry targeted the wrong person.

After that night in the task force office, I did not see Hapeta again, but a few months later I received a letter from an ex-prisoner who had just been released from Boggo Road gaol. The writer claimed to be a personal friend of Hector Hapeta and said in no uncertain terms that I was to blame for Hector being charged and I shouldn't have done it. I passed the letter to the Commission of Inquiry, but the person who read it told me not to take it too seriously, which was easy for him to say as it wasn't his family that was living in fear.

***

Soon after the Hapeta episode I travelled to the Gold Coast with another Brisbane detective to investigate allegations against two detectives of having stolen $4000 cash from a person they had arrested. The person claimed to have had the money stolen from him while he was in the watch-house. It was small beer compared with most of our investigations but it turned out that the complainant had something more interesting to tell us.

He said that despite having a criminal record he had applied for and been successful in getting a job at a luxury tourist resort in far north Queensland. He had been there only a short time when another employee came to speak to him. The way his colleague spoke left no doubt that he

AN UNDERCOVER OFFICER'S COVER IS BLOWN

had spent time in prison and that he had recognised our complainant as a fellow inmate. As a result of being recognised, our complainant was certain that he would lose his job at the resort. But the dismissal he was expecting never came. Meanwhile, he became more and more involved in the after-hours social activities of the staff.

As a keen swimmer he used to go to the beach every day, either before or after work, and it was here that he became friendly with 'Freddie', whose job it was to look after and hire out equipment for water sports. While they sat chatting beneath Freddie's sun umbrella, a steady trickle of guests would openly buy cocaine from Freddie. The source of the drug, he said, was two high-profile businessmen. Although they did not carry the cocaine themselves, their regular visits to the resort always coincided with an abundant new supply. Their visits were strictly business only and they never stayed more than a day and a night before leaving. According to our complainant, Freddie's cocaine business was common knowledge to the rest of the staff and to some local detectives, who ensured that the owners of the resort were warned well in advance of any visits by the police.

The information he gave us was consistent with information I obtained from other sources, including a police officer I knew to be honest who told me he suspected that some of the officers at his station were on the resort's payroll.

The investigation into the supposedly stolen $4000 went nowhere, but I took a long statement from the complainant about Freddie and his coke dealings and the local detectives he claimed were on the take. When I handed the statement to Huey, he told me, 'This statement is absolute dynamite. I'll pass this straight onto the inquiry.' But like many other allegations concerning corrupt police and drugs, the case was never followed up.

The situation at the Independent Task Force had been bad enough when there were two task forces; now there were three it was even worse. The cult of secrecy demanded by Huey meant that the right hand never knew what the left was doing. He received regular reports from the Commission of Inquiry but information rarely filtered down to other staff. Colleagues were starting to bicker and fight among themselves over trivial issues.

The inquiry was still making headlines but the public was becoming frustrated that Commissioner Fitzgerald had made so little progress with drugs, which to many Queenslanders—including me—was the most important issue of all. I will never stop believing that Fitzgerald would have been backed all the way if he had decided to go after the big drug dealers, but it was a can of worms and for whatever reason he chose not to open it.

By the end of 1988 the Commission of Inquiry was winding down. Huey and I were still at loggerheads and I had taken about as much as I could. I was desperate to get out.

On 4 November Phil Dickie, the investigative journalist who had broken the story of the illegal brothels operating in broad daylight under the noses of the police, launched his book, *The Road to Fitzgerald and Beyond*. Dickie's investigation of organised crime in Queensland won him Australian journalism's prestigious Walkley Award. In his foreword to the book the former Queensland police commissioner, Ray Whitrod, wrote: 'The honest people of Queensland, indeed of Australia, are under an obligation to Phil Dickie and his journalist colleagues who helped force the creation of an Inquiry.' Without Dickie I think nothing would have happened.

At about 10.15 a.m. Huey suggested that he and I and a detective sergeant attend the launch of Dickie's book at the Crest International Hotel. After the formalities Phil came up to me and asked if we could go somewhere quiet for a chat. We left the hotel and found a seat in a corner of King George Square. We spoke for some time about our hopes for the inquiry before saying goodbye and going our separate ways.

AN UNDERCOVER OFFICER'S COVER IS BLOWN

I went back to work and was about to enter my office when Huey yelled at the top of his voice, 'I want to see you right now.'

I could see the veins popping on his temples. He shouted, 'Have you been talking to Phil Dickie?'

I said I had. Huey was livid. He accused me of passing on confidential information, which was not true. What Dickie and I had talked about was the subject of gossip all over town.

There were quite a few staff around and most of them were scurrying for the lifts to get away from Huey's onslaught.

Just talking to a reporter was a crime in Huey's book. I denied leaking confidential information and insisted on going down to the inquiry to find out who had made the accusation against me. When I said that, Huey's manner quickly changed. He said, 'Cut it out, Col. I don't go in for these confrontations. Someone else pulled that one on me once before.'

I knew it was over, and that my time at the task force was over too. Huey calmed down but as I walked out of his office I could feel a pain in my left arm. I thought I was about to suffer my second heart attack. The next day I went to see my doctor, who said I was suffering from stress and gave me two weeks' sick leave. While I was at home Huey phoned to tell me that I had been promoted to the rank of senior sergeant and was to take charge of Woolloongabba police station. Huey also said, 'Forget about the Phil Dickie matter because I've forgotten about it and I won't raise it again.'

My last shift at the Independent Task Force was 23 December 1988. It was the end of what felt like a grim chapter in my policing career. I didn't respect Huey and I dare say he felt the same about me. We had rubbed each other the wrong way from the start. I felt bad to be leaving behind capable and enthusiastic young officers I had helped to recruit, but I couldn't have stood another day. I took two weeks' leave before taking up my new posting.

THIRTEEN

Hitting a brick wall

Woolloongabba police station dated from well before the turn of the century. It comprised two sections: the ground floor was for uniformed staff and the upper level was for the Criminal Investigation Branch (CIB). The station had a commanding presence due to its strategic location close to what has been historically known as the 'Gabba Five Ways', where five arterial roads merged.

As a result of the turmoil caused by the Fitzgerald Inquiry all promotions had been put on hold, but the retirement of the senior sergeant at the Gabba meant that somebody of my rank was needed to fill the vacancy. If it had been up to me I would not have chosen Woolloongabba, since I knew there were officers there, both uniformed and in the CIB upstairs, who held a grudge against me for having given evidence at the Commission of Inquiry. Two of the detectives were known as henchmen of the stood-down commissioner, Terry Lewis, and had been named by Jack Herbert at the inquiry as the recipients of bribes.

I had only been at the Gabba for a few days when I received the threatening letter from an ex-prisoner at Boggo Road gaol who was friends with Hector Hapeta. I knew that Hapeta himself was free on bail, which didn't make me sleep any easier, since my family was still unprotected.

I was working a late shift one evening when one of the young constables approached me and said, 'Senior, have you ever been upstairs for a look around? I think you should. Someone has dug up some newspaper articles about you and posted them all over the doors and walls. They have changed some of the words. What they have done is pretty offensive.'

It was after hours and there was nobody working the late shift upstairs so the young constable and I went for a look. To my absolute disgust I saw several articles relating to me that had been cut out of newspapers and posted up in the muster room. The captions and headlines on all of them had been altered with derogatory and insulting comments.

I thanked the young constable for telling me about it as by doing so he risked making enemies of the detectives who had been named before the Commission of Inquiry. I raised the matter the next day with the superintendent and told him that I wanted something done about it. He asked me to accompany him to the office of the detective inspector in charge of the CIB to confront him about the issue. I knew this particular fellow by sight but we had never been introduced. I was well aware that he was a close mate of Terry Lewis.

The superintendent didn't mince his words but the detective inspector treated the whole thing as a joke. I looked him in the eye and said, 'I reckon I know the fellows who did it and I might have to ask them to step outside.'

'Good idea,' the inspector replied. 'We could probably take a book on it.' The smug look on his face told me everything I needed to know about how seriously he took my complaint.

HITTING A BRICK WALL

The superintendent turned to me and said, 'Col, you're entitled to have a formal investigation into this matter and if that's what you want I'll set the wheels in motion.'

I knew he was sincere but a formal investigation was the last thing I wanted. The Queensland Police Force was being turned inside out by the Commission of Inquiry and it wouldn't have served any good purpose to have a whole CIB being investigated on a disciplinary matter. In any case I had been in the police force long enough to know that any investigation into my complaint would have been an exercise in futility. I had made my point and I told the superintendent I was prepared to let the matter rest.

I thought my bad experiences at the Independent Task Force were behind me but that turned out to be wishful thinking. After I had been at the Gabba for a couple of months I received a call from Huey. He told me that a journalist from one of the Brisbane TV stations wanted to interview someone at the task force about allegations made by one of my informants concerning large-scale drug importations. The informant had since vanished without a trace. Huey told me that in his position he couldn't give an interview and asked me if I would be prepared to do it.

I didn't buy Huey's reasons for not doing the interview himself but I told him I didn't mind. The journalist contacted me and I agreed to speak to him at Woolloongabba police station. We discussed at length the possible whereabouts of the informant and whether he had gone into hiding or been made to disappear. The journalist arranged with me to do an on-camera interview to generate public interest and hopefully to help find the missing informant.

I gave Huey the details and he gave the all-clear and said he would make one of his interview rooms available. The interview was scheduled for 12.45 p.m. the following day, 2 March 1989, at the headquarters of the Independent Task Force.

CODE OF SILENCE

The next day, just after 10 a.m., Huey rang me at home and told me the interview was off. He had run the matter past Bob Needham, his boss at the Commission of Inquiry, who told him that the guidelines had been changed and this particular matter was now deemed too sensitive to be made public. It was left to me to contact the journalist and tell him that the interview had been cancelled. Nothing was ever said about it again, but it was further evidence of the shambolic way the police force functioned in the wake of the Fitzgerald Inquiry.

The personal satisfaction I had once felt at being a part of the process that exposed the corruption inside the Queensland Police Force had long since vanished. My reward for having the courage to break the code of silence was to be constantly looking over my shoulder; to be abused at work and harassed and threatened by people who didn't have the courage to show their faces. I'd suffered one heart attack already and my career showed every sign of hitting a brick wall. So when a producer from Southern Star Sullivan rang me at home one night and asked whether I would consider playing myself in a television series about the Fitzgerald Inquiry, I didn't exactly leap for joy. The past year had brought me nothing but trouble and she was offering me the chance to relive it. I could imagine what the reaction would be at Police Headquarters. John Huey kicking and punching the lockers was nothing compared with what the police executive would do when they found out that the whole nightmare of the Fitzgerald Inquiry was going to be replayed on national television—and that one of their own officers was going to take part!

* * *

The series was to be called *Police State* and would be a dramatised documentary. The producer told me who would be in the cast and which characters each of them would be playing. Graeme Parker was to be played by Bill Hunter. Nick Tate was a dead ringer for the part of Commissioner Fitzgerald. The director was Chris Noonan, who went on to direct the hit movie *Babe*.

My first question was, why didn't they just use an actor? She explained that they had checked all the agencies and couldn't find an Indigenous actor who looked anything like me. She also told me that Actor's Equity had agreed to waive the usual requirement to hire a union member if I agreed to play the part. Finally, she offered to write to the acting commissioner of police to get his approval for me to appear. I said that was a bad idea because the acting commissioner was certain to say no. I didn't want to talk about money so I told her I would think about it and get back to her the next day.

Against my better judgement, I was tempted. Linda, however, was dead against it. She thought I had got myself into enough hot water already. She warned me that as soon as the acting commissioner got to hear of it, he'd sack me.

I didn't want to make matters worse than they already were, but at the same time I felt that Linda was overreacting. I had been persona non grata with most of the powers that be since the day I decided to give evidence. Virtually nobody above inspector would risk being seen talking to me for fear it would harm their career prospects. If there was anything stopping the police executive from sending me out to Longreach or Mount Isa where I couldn't do any harm, it was probably the fact that the media knew who I was and supported me. The media were on my side and I wanted to keep them that way.

I rang the producer the next day and said I'd take the part. I made it clear that I didn't want to be paid, except for my out-of-pocket expenses. The film was going to be shot in Sydney and the producer estimated that I would be needed for two days, for which I could use rostered days off.

The producers wanted everything to be accurate, so I had to smuggle my police uniform to Sydney. (This in itself was a breach of departmental rules, since I had no authority to wear my Queensland police uniform in New South Wales.) Much of the film was shot outside. I spent the whole two days praying I wouldn't be recognised. As I stood in my uniform on some of Sydney's busiest streets, I was in dread of being spotted by one of my New South Wales counterparts. On a couple of occasions I did notice a police car drive past as we were filming and I'm certain they would have noticed the strange uniform.

One morning I was chatting with a group of hired extras when one of them said, 'Which agency are you with?'

As I tried to think of an answer, another of the extras piped up, 'He's not an extra, he's the real thing.' I froze. Suddenly there were a dozen extras firing questions at me about the Fitzgerald Inquiry, wanting to know whether other police were giving me a hard time and whether I thought I had any future in the Queensland Police Force. I told them I didn't know.

While the producers had me down in Sydney they organised an interview with a journalist from the *Bulletin* magazine. Somehow the assurance of getting official authorisation had gone out the window, but I was past caring. I knew that when the *Bulletin* article hit the streets I'd be in more strife with the police hierarchy, but as far as I was concerned I had nothing to lose.

***

The story of the inquiry was still unfolding, so the final minutes of *Police State* were not to be put together until the last possible minute. It was announced by the ABC in advance that the program would not be screened in Queensland, but hundreds of videotapes must have winged their way to Brisbane the next day. As I predicted, I received plenty of

HITTING A BRICK WALL

flak for both the *Bulletin* article and *Police State*, but by now the hierarchy had something more urgent to worry about.

On Monday, 3 July 1989, just over a fortnight after *Police State* had gone to air, Commissioner Fitzgerald handed down his long-awaited report. It was an historic event and Queenslanders had looked forward to it with a mixture of elation and dread. I know that I was not the only one to feel disappointed, not by what the report contained but by what it left out. Fitzgerald's failure to follow the trail of drugs through the parlours baffled me then and it still baffles me. On the positive side, the release of the report helped shake the police force out of the paralysis that had gripped it since the inquiry began.

The special state prosecutor, Doug Drummond QC, was busy trying to establish prima facie cases and refer criminal charges against corrupt police, politicians and others named in the report. After two years during which promotions and transfers had been put on hold, the Queensland Police Force started advertising vacancies for senior ranks.

The list of vacancies was published in the Queensland *Police Gazette* as well as in the major newspapers. There were 30 or 40 vacancies for the rank of inspector. When I studied the requirements for the commissioned officer vacancies I felt confident that my background and experience in operational policing, both in uniform and plain clothes, would give me a strong chance of reaching the interview stage. If I'd had a crystal ball I would have known that I was wasting my time even applying.

Weeks went by without any word from the selection panel but I wasn't overly concerned as I knew that hundreds would be applying for promotion and that sooner or later I would be interviewed.

Finally the list of promotions was published in the *Courier Mail*. My name was not on the list—how could it be when I hadn't even been interviewed, let alone shortlisted?

One of my siblings phoned to tell me that Mum had been so excited when she opened the newspaper that she thought she must have missed my name among the promotions, so she read the whole list again. When she realised that my name wasn't there, she dropped the newspaper and retired to her bedroom.

Being turned down for promotion was a crushing blow. It wouldn't have been so bad if I had been shortlisted and passed over, but they hadn't even considered me worth interviewing. What hurt me more was that some of the new inspectors were junior to me in service by a decade or even more. Many had negligible operational experience and some had never even been to court to give evidence under oath in defended cases.

I know that I was not the only one surprised by my failure to get a promotion. I was asked by some of my staff at the Gabba and by other colleagues whether I had applied for any of the commissioned officer positions. When I told them that I had put in for several positions but had not even been interviewed they were absolutely dumbfounded. I tried not to show it, but I was devastated. While I still had a job, my career seemed over.

After the initial wave of promotions, a panel was set up to provide feedback to those like me who had applied for promotion but missed out. Before long I was called up to Police Headquarters. My interview was conducted by Assistant Commissioner Ron McGibbon, who eventually became a deputy commissioner and whom I had never laid eyes on until that day. He didn't bother with any small talk but went straight to the point. He said, 'You have recently made application for several positions for promotion to the rank of inspector and of course you were unsuccessful.'

I said, 'I wasn't even interviewed.'

He replied, 'You need a lot more development before you think about applying for your next promotion.'

HITTING A BRICK WALL

That was all he said. I waited for some helpful feedback that might improve my chances next time but there wasn't any. Not a word. I had the feeling that the only reason for bringing me in was to cut me down to size. The message about my missed promotion came across loud and clear: it seemed to me this was payback time.

***

It now dawned on me that Woolloongabba was just about the worst place I could have been transferred to. The Gabba was just a few minutes by car from the illegal casinos and massage parlours of Fortitude Valley. Anyone who wanted to have a go at me could come and find me in their lunch hour! Realising I'd been stitched up, I decided to phone the office of the commissioner of police for an appointment to ask the acting commissioner if it was possible to be relocated to a safer working environment.

By this time Ron Redmond had retired as acting commissioner, which was unfortunate for me because Redmond had always treated me with respect. He had been replaced by a superintendent. When I got through to the office of the commissioner I spoke to a young sergeant named Dave with whom I had always got along. After Dave put me on hold, another male voice come on the line and started screaming abuse at me, demanding to know who the f ... I thought I was, phoning the commissioner's office and expecting an appointment to see the commissioner.

The man, I found out later, held the same rank—senior sergeant—as me.

When he had finished shrieking, I shot back, 'Forget it. I am going to report this conversation.' I slammed the phone down on its cradle but almost immediately it started ringing. The senior sergeant had panicked and called the acting commissioner, Brian Pitman, who knew me quite well. He could tell at once how upset I was. 'Col,' he said, 'I want you to take a few minutes to calm down and then come in to see me.'

'You don't know what upset is,' I said. 'That bastard is a disgrace to his uniform. I should come in and sort him out right now.'

'Come on, Col,' said Pitman. 'That won't do any good.'

'I am at the end of my tether,' I said. 'I won't tolerate what just happened to me from him or from anyone else. I'll be in your office in half an hour.'

Pitman shook my hand when I arrived and said, 'I want you to calm down, Col.' He forced the senior sergeant to apologise for the way he had spoken to me but there was no sincerity in it.

We went into Pitman's office and he shut the door. My hopes of a sympathetic hearing were soon dashed. It was obvious that he didn't get what the problem was. I could tell from the look on his face that he thought I was being melodramatic. He probably took it for granted that my family and I were under witness protection and didn't see what else needed to be done.

After I had finished speaking he shrugged his shoulders and said, 'Col, if we move you now, what happens in another three months? Will we have to look at shifting you again?'

I was speechless. I looked at him and thought, 'This is it. They've washed their bloody hands of me.'

FOURTEEN

The most unwanted job in the police force

Two days after I walked out of the assistant commissioner's office I got a call at work from my namesake, Col Dillon, who was still receiving intimidating phone calls meant for me. He said, 'Col, I don't wish to alarm you but my wife received a telephone call only a couple of minutes ago and a male caller said to her "We have your daughter" before hanging up. I know where our daughter is and I know she is safe so I immediately thought of you. I don't know whether or not you have a daughter but if you do, I think you should check that she is safe.'

I dropped what I was doing and drove straight to my daughter's school, where I told the principal what had happened and asked him to tell Sandra's teacher that under no circumstances should Sandra be allowed outside the school grounds until she was collected either by me or by my wife. Needless to say, I didn't bother reporting the incident to the police. They had laughed off the threat

I received from Hector Hapeta's gaol buddy, so I had no reason to think they would take a threat against my daughter any more seriously.

In early March 1990 I was contacted by a senior adviser to the Minister for Police and Emergency Services, Terry Mackenroth, who wanted to talk to me about possible compensation for what had happened to me since giving evidence to the Commission of Inquiry.

Until now I hadn't thought about compensation; I was more concerned about getting my career back on track. But I had to face the fact that I had been in poor health ever since my heart attack and that eventually I might be forced to take early retirement. I still had a mortgage to pay and my children hadn't finished their education.

* * *

When I went to talk to the adviser he began by telling me that he felt a compensation claim made by another officer was excessive. From the way he spoke I got the impression that it was up to the adviser, rather than the minister, whether, and how much, compensation was to be paid.

We didn't discuss the specifics of my case but he advised me that legislation would have to be drafted to get the ball rolling and he promised to keep me informed. On my way out I briefly met Mackenroth but he didn't even bother asking how I was.

As it turned out, I need not have worried about being left at the Gabba. On 21 September 1990 I was seconded to the new Police Headquarters at 100 Roma Street, just around the corner from the old headquarters in Makerston Street, with the rank of senior sergeant. (A month later I was made acting inspector.) I reported to Chief Superintendent John Banham, who had been given the daunting task of setting up the new Professional Standards Unit to replace the hopelessly ineffective Internal Investigations Branch. This was one of

THE MOST UNWANTED JOB IN THE POLICE FORCE

the first major reforms to the Queensland Police Force (now renamed the Queensland Police Service or QPS) to be put into effect in the aftermath of the Fitzgerald Inquiry.

Chief Superintendent Banham was honest, capable and loyal—qualities that were in short supply in most of the bosses I had previously worked for. He had a reputation as a 'hatchet man'—a reputation which in my opinion was undeserved but which Banham seemed to quite enjoy. He had certainly made a name for himself as a safe pair of hands and was exactly the right man to be put in charge of an outfit like the Professional Standards Unit.

In the beginning the unit was given virtually no resources. We rustled up a big desk and two borrowed chairs and planted ourselves in the corner of a large open-plan office. I'm not sure we even had our own telephone.

Hundreds of internal disciplinary files had accumulated over many decades, a legacy of the abolished and discredited Internal Investigations Unit. Our first task was to plough through these files in order to produce reports on the numerous police who had been the subject of investigations. In many cases there was abundant prima facie evidence of flawed investigations into allegations of corrupt or unethical police work, which was hardly surprising, given the way the police had operated. The code of silence and the cult of not dobbing on a fellow police officer made it virtually impossible for one detective to investigate charges against another, even if he wanted to (and most didn't). Those who attempted to investigate their colleagues without fear or favour were no doubt stymied either by blind loyalty or by fear of retribution. As a result the old Internal Investigations Unit was a toothless tiger that served no worthwhile purpose. Instead of rooting out corruption and unethical behaviour in the police force it condoned and encouraged them. The proof of it was in those boxes of disciplinary files.

CODE OF SILENCE

Anyone who thought the Queensland Police Force would be transformed overnight was kidding themselves. The old guard was determined to hang on. One morning Superintendent Banham told me he was going to a meeting at the Police Operations Centre. As he walked out of the door I said facetiously, 'Make sure you say hello to my mate Darcy.'

'Don't you two get along?' asked Chief Superintendent Banham.

'You could say that,' I replied. 'Buckley hates, loathes and detests me.'

Banham beckoned me to follow him out of the main office into the atrium, where our conversation would not be overheard. He told me he had seen Buckley the previous day and that Buckley had said, 'What's Col Dillon doing up there on the seventh floor [where the commissioner's office was]? How's he going on the Scotch?'

When Superintendent Banham asked him what he meant, Buckley replied, 'Just ask Col how he's going on the Scotch.'

I didn't ask Superintendent Banham what he thought about Buckley but I had the feeling that he had no great respect for him. It wouldn't have been appropriate for me to tell him everything I knew about Buckley so I said nothing. But I knew exactly what Buckley was alluding to: it was a reference to the bottle of Chivas Regal that Harry Burgess had put in my locker on behalf of Ann Marie Tilley, and that was now in the possession of the Commission of Inquiry as Exhibit number 194. Obviously Buckley was in on it too; they all were. Mentioning it to Chief Superintendent Banham was a typically underhanded thing for Buckley to do, but it showed that the old culture was still going strong and that haters like Buckley were never going to give me any peace.

It was disheartening for me to see Buckley progressing up the promotional ladder when my career had come to a standstill. As far as I could tell he had withheld information about

THE MOST UNWANTED JOB IN THE POLICE FORCE

Parker from the inquiry and got away scot-free. Obviously he had connections who were looking out for him, which was more than I had.

The support I received always came more from outside the force than inside. One afternoon I was walking to my car in the basement car park under Police Headquarters when someone called out to me, 'Hey there, have you got a minute?'

I turned around and saw a man walking towards me who would have filled the entire front row of an A-grade rugby league team. He had a large square jaw and bushy black eyebrows. I recognised him at once from pictures I had seen in the newspapers: it was Carl Mengler, who been headhunted from Victoria to lead the police contingent attached to the newly established Criminal Justice Commission (CJC). Mengler had investigated the Griffith mafia as part of the Donald Mackay murder case and arrived in Queensland with a fearsome reputation as a crime and corruption fighter. He introduced himself and shook my hand and said, 'I know who you are. I have heard a great deal about you and you are one hell of a guy. I hope your police force appreciates what you've done and is looking after you.'

We were both in a hurry and I didn't want to burden him with my problems, but for me it was par for the course. With a few exceptions like Chief Superintendent Banham, the only respect I ever seemed to get was from outsiders. My own police force didn't want to know me.

The Labor Government under Wayne Goss was already looking for another police commissioner, the third since Terry Lewis had been sacked just three years earlier. The current commissioner, Noel Newnham, was a good man and I hoped he would survive but the word was already going round that Jim O'Sullivan, who was then Assistant Commissioner for the North Coast Region, was being groomed for the job. Newnham was a reformer who had been imported from Victoria to clean up the Queensland Police but the Queensland Police Union wanted him out and they usually got their wish. (Back in 1976 the union had got rid of another reforming commissioner, Ray Whitrod—his replacement was Terry Lewis.)

While seconded to the Commission of Inquiry, O'Sullivan had been in charge of the Witness Protection Unit, which had spent millions of dollars of taxpayers' money protecting corrupt police like Jack Herbert but couldn't even save my family from abusive phone calls. O'Sullivan and I had met only once but O'Sullivan didn't have a clue who I was.

If the rumours were true and O'Sullivan was going to take over from Newnham as police commissioner, I couldn't see things getting much better for me. I knew that Newnham had a battle on his hands but he was my best hope of obtaining the promotion I felt I deserved, and of gaining some recognition for my role in exposing corruption.

I wrote a long report explaining the stand I had taken and outlining the persecution I had suffered as a result of giving evidence to the Commission of Inquiry. I then hand-delivered it to the Office of the Commissioner in an envelope marked 'Personal and Confidential'. To my surprise I was met by the deputy commissioner instead of one of the staff. There was little in the way of conversation but I was taken aback when he said to me, 'I hope you haven't painted yourself into a corner.'

I didn't ask him what he meant but his remark left me with an uneasy feeling that he had been party to some discussion about me and that I was wasting my time.

Three days later I received an envelope marked 'Personal and Confidential' and personally signed by Commissioner Newnham. The letter acknowledged that I had been badly treated and invited me to apply for any future advertised positions for which I felt that I possessed the necessary prerequisites. It was an uplifting letter and it gave me hope that

THE MOST UNWANTED JOB IN THE POLICE FORCE

I would be treated honestly and impartially when applying for promotion, which was all I asked. I didn't want any favours, just the chance to be assessed fairly on my merits.

***

Investigating other police is the most unwanted job in the police force and nobody was in a hurry to join the Professional Standards Unit. It didn't matter whether it was called Professional Standards or Internal Investigations—the rest of the police force treated you like a leper. It was a fact of life that, as a member of the Professional Standards Unit, whenever you walked into the cafeteria at headquarters you never had to wait in the queue because other police would disperse in a matter of seconds, leaving you alone at the head of the queue. Colleagues would never contemplate dropping in for a social visit for fear that if they were seen entering the Professional Standards Unit it would be interpreted that they were under investigation or—even worse—that they were there for the purpose of dobbing on other police.

I had been at the Professional Standards Unit for less than six months when a vacancy came up for the position of inspector. As I was only an acting inspector, I needed to apply for promotion in order to secure a permanent position. By this time I had come to know my boss, Chief Superintendent John Banham, quite well. He was a straight shooter and I enjoyed working for him.

The selection panel consisted of Banham himself, two inspectors and a more senior officer. My heart sank when I realised this high-ranking officer would be sitting on my panel because I had only just carried out a departmental investigation on his son, a mid-ranking officer who worked in one of the regions. My recommendation after examining all the evidence was that the son should be departmentally disciplined and probably demoted.

The senior officer far outranked Chief Superintendent Banham. His questioning bordered on the hostile but Banham and the other two inspectors were firmly on my side. The result of the interview was that I was promoted to commissioned rank—subject to any appeals. I found out that three appeals had been lodged against my promotion to inspector; in order for the promotion to be confirmed I had to win all three.

The appeals process was handled by a single public service commissioner for appeals who operated independently from the main selection process. I was confident of seeing off two of the appellants as my experience of operational policing was far wider than theirs. The third officer, however, had an impressive operational record. It was up to the appeals commissioner to decide which of us to promote.

We were kept waiting for a fortnight. Finally I received a telephone call asking me to report to the office of a chief superintendent whom I had never met before. I discovered that he worked for the appeals commissioner and was responsible for the processing of promotions. He handed me a document to sign which confirmed that I was ready to accept my promotion to the rank of inspector of police at the Professional Standards Unit. With a wry grin on his face he shook my hand and said, 'No doubt you'll be more than happy to sign this document.'

The date was 14 January 1991, an important date for me and a milestone in my life and my policing career. I was now an inspector of police. Instead of going back to my office, I found a small conference room that nobody was using and sat alone with my thoughts in the darkness. I thought about my father and the lessons he had taught me, to act honestly and to have the courage of my convictions. It was the values I had absorbed from him that gave me the strength to give my evidence at the Commission of Inquiry. If he could have told me what the consequences would be, not just for me but

THE MOST UNWANTED JOB IN THE POLICE FORCE

for Linda and the children, would he still have wanted me to speak out? I was sure he would and that, in my position, he would have done the same. As an Indigenous man, my father experienced racism throughout his life. Sitting there in the dark, I was proud to think that I was the first Indigenous man to be promoted to commissioned rank in any police force in Australia.

After I had pulled myself together I went back to my office. The staff had gone home and only Chief Superintendent Banham remained. When I told him that my promotion had come through he reached out and shook my hand. The expression on his face said it all. I knew that he was genuinely happy for me, and also that I might never have got there without the support and guidance he had given me. Banham was one of very few people I'd met who knew how to counsel me out of my natural pigheadedness and to show me that there might be more than one solution to a problem.

In the course of conversation Chief Superintendent Banham pointed out that I would need to go and buy myself a mess jacket since I would be expected to join the officers' mess. 'Col,' he said, 'you've got to understand that from here on it's all political and you have to play the game.'

I knew Banham was right but I'd seen enough of police politics—the shameless sucking up to high-ranking officers, the desperate attempts to get noticed by the commissioner at social events—to know that it wasn't for me. I told him straight away that I wouldn't be joining the officers' mess. He didn't say anything but I could guess what he was thinking.

Unbeknown to me, Commissioner Newnham and his deputy, David Blizzard, had set the wheels in motion for me to be formally recognised for my services to policing in the state of Queensland and recommended that I be given an award.

As with all potential recipients, extensive checks had to be done into my background and career record to determine my general suitability and whether or not I had fulfilled the specific requirements of the award. Although Newnham and Blizzard would have known a little about my policing background, they took what they believed to be the appropriate steps by referring their report and nomination to Assistant Commissioner Jim O'Sullivan. O'Sullivan was a logical choice since he had been in charge of the police and witness protection contingent during the Fitzgerald Inquiry and he would have had a detailed knowledge of my role. On the other hand, O'Sullivan knew nothing about me personally because I had never worked under him. After reading the report, he gave his comments in a short handwritten note in which he stated that I was not deserving of an award because all I had done was what I should have been doing and that was simply my duty.

How do I know this? I was told it by a young sergeant who was a staff member in the deputy commissioner's office. It was his job to register and sort out correspondence in order of priority before delivering it to the deputy commissioner. He was the first to read O'Sullivan's comments when they arrived at the office. He told me that Deputy Commissioner Blizzard had been furious and went to see Commissioner Newnham and that the two of them had decided to press on with my nomination for an award regardless of O'Sullivan's remarks.

I was at a complete loss to understand O'Sullivan's hostility towards me. We had barely spoken a dozen words to each other. All I could think was that O'Sullivan was one of the old guard and he blamed me, rather than the police taking bribes, for having thrown the force into turmoil.

***

Noel Newnham did not survive much longer as commissioner. The Labor Government and the police union both wanted him out. By the end of 1992 he was gone, another reformer hounded out of a job.

THE MOST UNWANTED JOB IN THE POLICE FORCE

The obvious frontrunner to replace Newnham as commissioner of police was O'Sullivan, who had been all but anointed to the job by Fitzgerald. On page 338 of his report, Fitzgerald wrote:

> Special mention is warranted with reference to Detective Inspector James Patrick O'Sullivan. This officer jeopardised his career when he accepted the appointment as the senior police officer seconded to assist this Commission in the circumstances which then existed and served in that role with distinction throughout the Inquiry.
>
> Inspector O'Sullivan is 50 years of age, and his immediate promotion to the senior grade within the rank of Superintendent would be fitting recognition of his contribution to the Police Force and not discordant having regard to the ages of other Superintendents.

O'Sullivan was nominated by Fitzgerald as the person best qualified to vet nominations for the post of commissioner after Terry Lewis was sacked. Many suspected (rightly, as it happened) that it was only a matter of time before he became commissioner himself.

Before O'Sullivan was appointed commissioner, officers serving in the Professional Standards Unit had unrestricted daily access to the commissioner's office. This was natural given the nature of the work that we were doing. It was standard practice for Chief Superintendent Banham (he had recently been promoted) or another senior member of the unit to start the day by briefing Deputy Commissioner Blizzard on the progress of reports that were required by Blizzard before disciplinary proceedings could begin.

The day after O'Sullivan became commissioner, I was taken aside by the head of security at Police Headquarters and told that O'Sullivan had barred all members of the

Professional Standards Unit from entering his office. 'Sorry, Col,' he said, 'but from now on your security pass to the commissioner's office is invalid.' He asked me to break the news to Chief Superintendent Banham. When I told Banham, he thought I was joking. Assistant commissioners all over the state were already complaining about the time it was taking to complete disciplinary investigations. Officers under investigation were being stood down from their duties for long periods, and the situation would only get worse if the commissioner blocked us from submitting our reports.

The big loser under the new regime was Deputy Commissioner Blizzard who, like Newnham, had come from Victoria. Blizzard had a reputation as a disciplinarian and a reformer. The police union disliked Blizzard almost as much as it disliked Newnham.

Soon after O'Sullivan took over, we were verbally advised that we were no longer to deal with Deputy Commissioner Blizzard's office and that all operational and policy matters were to be handled by the office of the commissioner via his chief of staff. Blizzard, who had played such an active role under Commissioner Newnham, found himself sidelined.

One day I noticed Blizzard sitting alone in his office. He looked pretty miserable. I stopped and asked him what was going on.

'Col,' he said, 'I can't tell you much, but I will say this: O'Sullivan doesn't want me as his deputy and is trying to get rid of me. I came to Queensland to do a job and I intend to do just that. I won't go without a fight.'

'Hang in there, deputy,' I said. 'Nobody around here [meaning the Professional Standards Unit] wants to see you go.'

He said, 'Don't put yourself at risk by being seen talking to me.'

'Don't worry about me,' I said. 'I talk to who I please. O'Sullivan has very little time for me already and the feeling is mutual.'

THE MOST UNWANTED JOB IN THE POLICE FORCE

With Newnham gone, Blizzard had lost his most important ally. The strain began to tell and he was forced to take sick leave. It wasn't long before O'Sullivan moved to dismiss Blizzard as his deputy.

Blizzard lived close to me. I could understand how isolated he felt, so one evening I called round to offer him some moral support. While I was there Blizzard told me that a few days earlier he had been summoned to the commissioner's office and told by O'Sullivan to consider his options as there was no place for him in his administration. O'Sullivan then accused him of being disloyal and of having gone around making disparaging comments behind his back. Blizzard responded by telling O'Sullivan that he had sold himself out in order to take Newnham's job. I couldn't imagine that going down well. Blizzard was adamant that he would not resign but he told me that the government could terminate his contract with only three weeks' notice. It was pretty clear that O'Sullivan had him over a barrel. As a mere inspector I couldn't offer him much in the way of practical help, but I assured him that a lot of people would be disgusted if he was forced out. He said he appreciated my support, but I could tell that he was very demoralised.

I was starting to wonder how much had really changed since the Fitzgerald Inquiry had closed its doors. A few corrupt police had been caught out, but the old guard still seemed to be in control.

One of the key recommendations of the Fitzgerald Report had been the setting up of the Criminal Justice Commission. The wording of the report was as follows:

> A new entity is recommended, to be known as the Criminal Justice Commission, (CJC). It will be permanently charged with the monitoring, reviewing, co-ordinating and initiating reform of the administration of criminal justice. It will

also fulfil those criminal justice functions not appropriately carried out by the police or other agencies.

Fitzgerald wanted an Official Misconduct Division within the CJC, whose job was to be 'responsible for independent investigations of any suspected official misconduct. It may investigate individual cases or conduct broader based inquiries'. As to personnel, he wrote:

> The Official Misconduct Division will be served by police seconded to it for appropriate finite periods and on guidelines to be established by the Criminal Justice Committee. Police serving with the Official Misconduct Division will be relieved of any obligation to obey, provide information to or account to any other police officer save police posted to the Official Misconduct Division.
>
> All secondments to serve in the Official Misconduct Division should be for a relatively short time of two to three years, and non-renewable save when necessary to complete particular investigations where continuity is essential.

It could not have been clearer that Fitzgerald did not trust the police to investigate corruption and that he wanted the CJC to operate at arm's length from the police service. But as far as I was concerned, it was simply a case of the same old guard working for a new organisation.

One morning I was standing in the main foyer at Police Headquarters when I saw one of the old guard detectives who had been prominently mentioned at the Fitzgerald Inquiry for having been on the payroll of the 'bagman', Jack Herbert. As he made his way through the foyer, he was welcomed like a returning hero by two other detectives, both of whom had been seconded to work as investigators at the CJC. They noticed me standing nearby, but my presence was certainly no deterrent to them as they joked and shook hands with their corrupt old mate.

On the day Deputy Commissioner Blizzard was sacked I happened to meet Commissioner O'Sullivan. It was late afternoon and I was leaving Police Headquarters just as he was entering. O'Sullivan wasn't in uniform but was dressed in a dark blue suit, white shirt and tie. He gave me the coldest stare I had ever received from another human being—and I had been on the receiving end of a few of those in my policing career. Neither of us spoke to each other but the fact that he was not in uniform made me suspect that he had just come from talking to the minister, no doubt about getting rid of Blizzard. When I got home I rang Chief Superintendent Banham and told him I thought Blizzard was gone. Banham said he hadn't heard anything. Two hours later he called me back and said, 'Your hunch was right, Col. I have just been told that Deputy Commissioner Blizzard has been sacked.'

* * *

Without Blizzard, I knew that life would only get harder for me. My insomnia had been getting worse but I hadn't gone to see a doctor because I was frightened of being put on sleeping tablets. I had got into the habit of lying there half alert for intruders and now I couldn't break it.

I lay awake one morning in the early hours with a dull pain in my chest. I could still feel the pain when I went to work that morning. Around mid-morning I left the office to go to a primary school in the northern suburbs to talk about 'stranger danger'. I always enjoyed visiting schools but this morning I felt terrible. As I spoke to the children I felt the pain getting worse.

Afterwards I drove back to my office. As I passed the Prince Charles Hospital it crossed my mind to call in for a check-up. It was nearly seven years since my first heart attack and on that occasion I had been lucky to get to hospital in time. But I told myself the pain would pass and kept on driving. I was sitting at my desk after lunch when one of my friends, an inspector named Carol, asked me if I wanted a cup of coffee.

When she came back with the coffee she said, 'Are you all right, Col? You don't look too good.'

I told her I'd been having chest pains since the night before.

'You're going straight to hospital,' she said.

Carol raced into Chief Superintendent Banham's office, grabbed a set of car keys and took me straight to Prince Charles Hospital where I should have had the common sense to have taken myself several hours earlier. I didn't want to arrive at the hospital in uniform so I asked Carol to stop at my home so I could change. 'All right, Col,' she told me, 'but make sure you leave the front door open. I don't want to have to kick it down.'

Two days later I had my second bout of coronary surgery.

When I eventually returned to work, I sat down and had a long chat with Chief Superintendent Banham. My job at the Professional Standards Unit was literally killing me and we agreed that I needed to find a less stressful place to work.

As it turned out there was a vacancy for an inspector to take charge of the Cultural Advisory Unit. Initially I wasn't keen as it felt like another step back from the operational policing that I had always loved. But I had to face the reality that I had made too many enemies as a result of giving evidence to the Fitzgerald Inquiry to be able to return to front-line policing. I knew that for every corrupt detective who had been sacked as a result of my evidence, there were 50 mates who hated my guts. I was tired of always looking over my shoulder. With Banham's support, I was seconded there and began work on 24 November 1993. My secondment was to continue until further notice. Little did I know but this was to be my last job in the police force.

FIFTEEN

An unbridgeable rift

The Queensland Police Force began operating under its own legislation on 1 January 1864. Consisting of around 150 men, the force was divided into the Metropolitan Police, Rural Police, Water Police and a separate Native Police. It is worth noting that it took another 130 years for the Queensland Police Force to have its first Indigenous commissioned officer.

When I took charge of the Cultural Advisory Unit the relationship between the Queensland Police and the Aboriginal and Torres Strait Islander community was nearly at rock bottom. There had been a number of controversial incidents which had culminated in violent clashes between the police and the Indigenous community.

One incident which was to have a devastating effect on police–Indigenous relations over many years was the death in custody of an Aboriginal youth named Daniel Yock on 7 November 1993. Daniel and a couple of his mates, also Indigenous, were walking along a street in West End, Brisbane minding their own business when they were stopped by police officers driving a paddy-wagon. Some conversation took place, as a result of which Daniel was arrested and put in the back of the paddy-wagon. He was left there for nearly an hour instead of being taken straight to the city watch-house (a five-minute drive) to be charged with whatever offence he had been arrested for.

It was an extremely hot day and while he was locked in the paddy-wagon, Daniel suffered a fit. He died before he could be attended to by paramedics. Daniel was the latest but sadly not the last Aboriginal person to die in police custody despite all the promises of reform made in the wake of the 1987 Royal Commission into Aboriginal Deaths in Custody.

Tension was mounting daily as police and the Aboriginal community awaited the findings of a full inquiry into the circumstances of Daniel Yock's death which was being conducted by Mr Lew Wyvill QC, acting chair of the Criminal Justice Commission (CJC).

There was a strong expectation in the Aboriginal community that the report would be a whitewash and that the police officers who had arrested Daniel and left him in the back of their paddy-wagon would be exonerated from blame in his death. This was exactly what happened. The police who arrested Daniel were criticised for the manner in which they acted when detaining him and for the delay in taking him to the city watch-house to be formally charged. But Wyvill found that there was insufficient evidence to recommend that charges be laid against them.

The death of Daniel Yock, and the failure of the CJC to find anyone to blame for his death, caused a wave of protests and demonstrations by citizens demanding justice for Daniel.

As inspector in charge of the Cultural Advisory Unit (CAU), I was in an invidious position. Many people, black as well as white, had interpreted my presence there as purely tokenistic. They regarded my transfer as a feeble and insincere attempt by the government and the Queensland Police to placate the Aboriginal community, whose anger at police persecution, especially of young black men, was reaching a flashpoint.

My appointment to the CAU wasn't at all favourably received by the Indigenous community, many of whom accused me of being a traitor and of selling out my own race. I knew before I took up the job that it was a controversial role, but sometimes it seemed like I just couldn't win. I was as hated as much for my efforts to improve relations between Indigenous people and the police as I had been for taking a stand against corruption in the Licensing Branch.

***

At the time I joined the CAU a departmental investigation was already under way into violent clashes between police and Aboriginal and Torres Strait Islanders which had occurred in Roma Street outside Police Headquarters on 17 November 1993, ten days after the death of Daniel Yock. This melee resulted in my predecessor and a sergeant being unofficially stood aside from their duties at the CAU and directed not to have any contact or involvement with the Aboriginal and Torres Strait Islander community. The investigation into the melee in Roma Street hinged on allegations made by a couple of detectives against my predecessor and his sergeant and on counter allegations by them against the two detectives.

Following a request from the deputy commissioner's office for a full appraisal of the CAU, I was asked for a detailed report on the unit's activities, which I submitted to on 23 December 1993. I was later complimented on the report but was told this is not what they were after.

When I was asked to do the report on the CAU, I suspected straight away that the executive expected me to criticise my predecessor and the sergeant for the way they were running the CAU and in particular for the way they had handled the Roma Street protest. They wanted an excuse to get rid of the two men from the CAU and they were going to use my report to do it. No doubt they thought I would jump at the chance to wrest the CAU from the inspector by writing an adverse report on him and his offsider to bolster my claim to be given the role permanently. If so, my report would have disappointed them because I found that the two men had been doing an effective job and that they enjoyed the confidence and support of the Aboriginal and Torres Strait Islander community. In fact, Aboriginals and Torres Strait Islanders were refusing to have anything to do with the CAU until both the inspector and the sergeant were formally reinstated. Both men had worked hard to establish trust with the Indigenous community and both were well respected for their efforts to forge a better relationship between the police and Indigenous Australians.

My understanding of what happened on 17 November was that the inspector and the sergeant had done their best to calm the situation after Indigenous marchers arrived at Roma Street to protest about the death of Daniel Yock. The two men subsequently made a complaint to the Professional Standards Unit alleging that two detectives who were standing in the public car park at the Transit Centre, well out of harm's way, were actively provoking the Indigenous protesters by throwing cans into the crowd.

To me it seemed that my predecessor and his sergeant were being made scapegoats for a riot incited by their own colleagues. I couldn't see how this could be in the spirit of the new standards of police accountability set out in the recommendations of the Fitzgerald Report.

As the pair awaited their disciplinary hearing, I happened to bump into them in the corridor. Both appeared very nervous. I asked them if they had arranged any representation

AN UNBRIDGEABLE RIFT

by their respective unions or if they had sought any legal advice. They told me they hadn't. I then asked who would be supervising their hearing (assuming it would be an assistant commissioner) and they told me that it was being dealt with by the deputy commissioner. Neither of them seemed to realise the implications of this. I had to remind them that in all disciplinary matters dealt with by the deputy commissioner, he had the discretion to either sack or demote the officers if they were found guilty.

I said, 'You're fully entitled to have legal representation or to be accompanied by a friend. Would you like me to accompany you to the hearing?'

They seemed grateful but replied, 'You don't need to stick your neck out for us. You've already been through enough trouble of your own.'

I said, 'It's no trouble for me to come and make sure that you are given a fair hearing.'

That afternoon we went to the office of a very senior officer for the hearing. My appearance was not announced simply because I had only decided to go at the last minute.

The officer entered the room carrying a huge pile of documents. I remember thinking that we were in for a very long hearing. As he placed the documents on the table in front of him, he looked at me and said, 'G'day, Col. I wasn't expecting to see you here but you're welcome to sit in and listen.'

I apologised for not having notified him earlier and said that I would like to speak on behalf of the two men. What he said next took my breath away. 'Col,' he said, 'it really doesn't matter what you have to say. I've already made up my mind on this one.'

The inspector and the sergeant looked gobsmacked. It didn't sound like an impartial hearing but more like a kangaroo court.

The senior officer then excused himself and left the room, returning almost immediately. He said he was going to take a few minutes to read some of the material before starting the hearing proper. This struck me as strange, since he had just told us that he had already made up his mind. He finished reading and was about to speak when his staff officer entered the room, whispered something in his ear and then left.

We waited on tenterhooks to hear his decision, only to be told that something important had come up and he would have to adjourn the hearing, which would have to be rescheduled to another date.

As it turned out, the rescheduled hearing never took place and the matter was never mentioned again. Maybe the powers that be had a change of heart.

***

After the Roma Street melee the police force had to devise contingency plans to deal with future demonstrations in order to make sure it had the necessary manpower and resources. The heads of specialist sections began a series of meetings chaired by the deputy commissioner to plan for future demonstrations by the Aboriginal community over the death of Daniel Yock. Either deliberately or inadvertently, I was left out of these meetings. It was only by chance one morning that I found out that the next meeting was to be held in the commissioner's boardroom at Police Headquarters. I made sure I was there.

When I opened the door to the boardroom, the deputy commissioner was speaking. All eyes turned to look at me. He stopped in mid-sentence. 'I'm sorry, Col,' he said. 'You should have been notified. It won't happen again.'

I didn't believe for a second that it was an oversight.

One of the officers present at the meeting whom I'd known for many years approached me afterwards and expressed his dismay at the failure to notify me. To me, it was proof that I was regarded by Commissioner O'Sullivan's

AN UNBRIDGEABLE RIFT

shiny new Queensland Police Service as little more than a nuisance.

The death in custody of Daniel Yock had created what seemed like an unbridgeable rift between police and the Indigenous community, but there would be other damning incidents in the years ahead. As the officer-in-charge of the CAU I tried my best to improve relationships and open new lines of communication, but it felt like a losing battle.

At Ipswich Mall a violent clash broke out between police and the Indigenous community after the police arrested a number of Aboriginal people who were travelling from Rockhampton to the Aboriginal community of Woorabinda to attend a funeral. Most of the people arrested en route to Woorabinda had been detained for relatively minor offences such as outstanding warrants for traffic breaches. Although I was the inspector-in-charge of the CAU, I was never formally consulted about the proposed police action—if I had been, I would have strongly advised against the action in order to prevent further damage to the already poor relationship between police and the Indigenous community.

The Ipswich Mall incident demonstrated a lack of compassion and sensitivity in the behaviour of police on the ground and highlighted a more serious failure of leadership, from the commissioner down. The police and the Indigenous community, especially young men, were still locked in the old 'them and us' mentality and from the police side it seemed as if nothing would ever change.

In May 1994 three Aboriginal children aged twelve and upwards were picked up by six police in Brisbane's Fortitude Valley and driven in three police cars to a remote location at the mouth of the Brisbane River called Pinkenba, where they allegedly terrorised the children until 4 a.m. This would become known as the 'Pinkenba Six' incident.

After being driven to Pinkenba the three boys were told to take off their thongs which police allegedly threw into the river. After taunting them about the risk of being bitten by venomous snakes and eaten by lions and tigers, the police drove away, leaving the three boys to find their own way home.

Six officers would eventually face charges of deprivation of liberty. All would be acquitted. An internal investigation recommended that the police officers involved in the Pinkenba incident be either dismissed or demoted, but Commissioner O'Sullivan refused. Instead, the officers were given twelve-month good behaviour orders. The reason that no harsher punishment was imposed was that the officers had 'suffered severe financial and personal hardship'.

When news of the Pinkenba incident first broke I knew it would only be a matter of time before a complaint was lodged by the Aboriginal Legal Service on the boys' behalf demanding an investigation by the Criminal Justice Commission. Like most other Queenslanders, I first heard about the incident on the television news. My reaction was one of intense anger that nobody in the upper echelons of the police had bothered to inform me. As head of the CAU, I knew there was a fair chance I would be contacted by the media and asked for my comments. I could also expect calls from leaders of the Aboriginal community wanting to know exactly what had happened and what they could reasonably expect and hope for in terms of a proper investigation.

After the story broke it was followed up by every media organisation. I was in my office at the Cultural Advisory Unit when I was contacted by a journalist from the Brisbane *Courier Mail*. He asked me whether I knew what action was going to be taken against the six officers involved and whether I was prepared to say anything about the issue.

Requests for comment usually came through the police media unit, so I asked him whether he had contacted the media unit and whether he had tried to get a comment from any of the senior executives.

AN UNBRIDGEABLE RIFT

He said, 'Col, I have tried everybody at the top, the commissioner, the deputy commissioner and a few of the assistant commissioners and I couldn't get through to any of them, they've all gone to ground. Even your media section had no comment to make and as you're in charge of the Cultural Advisory Unit I thought I'd try you.'

The sensible thing would probably have been for me to decline to comment as an internal investigation was already under way, or to refer him back to the commissioner. But I was disgusted by yet another incident of Aboriginal kids being mistreated by the police and by the determination of the police hierarchy to keep me out of the loop.

I told the reporter, 'Quite simply there has been a total breakdown in communication between the police service and the Aboriginal community which has existed since the tragic death of Daniel Yock last November. I have been excluded from talks and not kept informed on issues relating to the inquiry into Daniel's death.'

After a few moments' silence the reporter said, 'Col, are you sure you want to go on the record with those comments? You know that you'll be putting your head on the chopping block by speaking out. This could get you in real trouble.'

I said, 'All I've told you is the truth about how things stand between the police service and the Aboriginal community.'

'OK, Col,' he said. 'If you're sure.'

That evening the journalist contacted me at home. I assumed he would be wanting to clarify the points we had discussed earlier, but he was calling to make sure that I wasn't having second thoughts. He said, 'If there's anything you want to change, Col, just tell me and I'll do it.'

I told him I appreciated the call but I was happy to stand by what I had said that morning. He thanked me and told me not to hesitate to call him if the published article caused me any trouble from those at the top.

It was another sleepless night. I knew that when the commissioner read what I had said, he would choke on his breakfast.

***

On 18 May 1994 the *Courier Mail* published a story under the headline 'Key officer not told of Pinkenba'.

I read the article carefully on my way to work. The journalist had accurately recorded everything I told him the previous day. It was a long article and I knew it would be impossible for the police hierarchy to ignore what I had said. I guessed that my phone would already be running hot and thought there was every chance of a call from the commissioner's office, or even the office of the police minister, asking me to please explain.

Sure enough, as I walked along the corridor to my office I could hear my phone ringing. When I picked up the receiver a voice said, 'Col, it's Acting Superintendent Mick O'Brien here. I want you to report to me straight away in relation to some comments you made in an article in today's *Courier Mail*.'

I went directly to O'Brien's office. I found him sitting at his desk with his palms down, as if he was about to spring at me. Although we had both attended the same departmental course at the police college a year earlier, this was the first time we had really spoken.

O'Brien didn't engage in any conversation to break the ice but launched straight into the issue of my speaking to the media and making comments that he said had embarrassed the police service. He told me that my remarks had upset and angered both the commissioner and the police minister. He informed me that as acting superintendent currently in charge of the Police Operations Centre and the commissioner's spokesman after hours, he too did not appreciate the comments I had made to the *Courier Mail*.

AN UNBRIDGEABLE RIFT

Up to that point he was leading the conversation. I could see that he was uptight but he was managing to control his temper. But when I began to answer one of his questions he suddenly shouted at me, 'Don't think for one moment that I'm going to put up with your tantrums.'

I was shaken by the ferocity in his voice. In 29 years' service, during which I had never been departmentally charged or even reprimanded, I had never been spoken to like that by a senior officer. It seemed to me that he was trying to provoke a reaction that would give him grounds to have me demoted or dismissed.

'Excuse me,' I replied. 'I am not given to throwing tantrums and I take exception to your remark.'

His face was crimson and I was sure he was going to slam his fist on the desk. He yelled at me to call in an Inspector Graham Gronow who was in the office a few doors down. It was all I could do not to say, 'Bloody well go and get him yourself!'

According to protocol, Gronow should have been the first to question me. When he walked into the office I could see that this was the last place on earth that he wanted to be. He refused to look me in the eye and spent the whole time staring at the floor. While O'Brien ranted and raved, Gronow didn't say a word. My crime, according to O'Brien, was speaking to the media without permission—an offence for which he could have me departmentally charged for breaching the code of conduct. He didn't seem particularly interested in what I had said but only in the fact that I had spoken to a journalist. 'What about the risk of being misquoted?' he said. 'Didn't that ever cross your mind?'

I calmly told him that I had read the article and that every word attributed to me was accurate.

Before dismissing me, O'Brien said in a menacing tone, 'I want a full report from you on my desk by the end of the day.'

'That's out of the question,' I replied. 'I have meetings all day and won't have any time.'

'Well make sure it's on my desk by the end of tomorrow,' he said.

'Tomorrow I will be just as busy,' I said. 'I won't be able to meet your deadline.'

By now he was ready to blow his top. 'I'll give you until Friday,' he said. 'Make sure it's on my desk without fail.'

I returned to my office with every intention of writing the report, as it was a lawful direction and I had a duty to comply. Between meetings I started typing but after completing a couple of paragraphs I asked myself what I thought I was doing. I had certainly breached guidelines by speaking to the media without permission, but everything I had told the journalist from the *Courier Mail* was true. As a commissioned police officer I had a duty to comply with departmental policy, but as head of the Cultural Advisory Unit I also had a responsibility to help repair relations with the Indigenous community. To me, the Pinkenba incident was the last straw. If the commissioner wouldn't confront it, somebody else had to.

I decided not to write the report. I pulled the few paragraphs I had typed out of the typewriter and threw them in the waste paper basket.

That afternoon Inspector Gronow stopped by my office and said, 'Superintendent O'Brien wants to know about that report he asked you to do. How is it going?'

I replied, 'You can tell him from me it's coming along fine.'

He asked me again the next day and the day after that. Each time I gave him the same answer. Friday came around and I was expecting a phone call from Mick to come to his office with the report, but it didn't happen. Next week came and went and there was no further word from Mick or inquiries by Gronow on his behalf. I had called his bluff and got away with it. The matter was never raised with me again.

SIXTEEN

Whistleblowers

In August 1993 I was elected inaugural president of the Queensland Whistleblowers Action Group (WAG). It was something I really didn't need at that time in my life and I certainly didn't do myself any favours by agreeing to be president. It was a position that required me to make statements in support of whistleblowers while publicly criticising government agencies for their attempts to stop employees from making public interest disclosures and to punish them for having done so. I knew from my own bitter experience the personal repercussions and career setbacks lying in wait for whistleblowers in the state of Queensland.

Needless to say, one of the targets of my criticism was the Queensland Police Service. My comments on behalf of the WAG did not endear me to the commissioner or the minister. I was told that a regular topic of conversation at Police Headquarters was what they could do to shut me up.

In my role as the president of the WAG I often put myself in breach of departmental policy for speaking out on issues involving the police. Whenever I made a statement to the media on such issues, the news article would invariably begin with the words 'The president of the Queensland Whistleblowers Action Group, Inspector Col Dillon, said yesterday . . .'.

The membership of the WAG consisted of men and women from all walks of life and included police officers, lawyers, doctors, nurses, teachers, scientists and many others. I am still a member today. I have known people whose careers have been destroyed and whose lives have been ruined as a result of their speaking out about corruption and mismanagement. One of the most important roles of the WAG was to provide support for whistleblowers subjected to harassment and victimisation by employers, colleagues and investigative agencies.

In the first eighteen months of its existence the WAG, through the unstinting efforts of its inaugural secretary, Eric Thorne, became one of the most effective public interest groups in Queensland. Some of its most notable achievements included presenting written and/or verbal submissions to the following bodies: the Senate Select Committee Inquiry into Public Interest Whistleblowing (August 1994); the Criminal Justice Commission (May 1974); the full shadow cabinet of the Queensland Government (August 1994); the Parliamentary Justice Committee Triennial Review of the CJC and the Senate Select Committee of Inquiry into Unresolved Whistleblower Cases (February 1995).

On one occasion I was approached by ABC Television's *7.30 Report* to appear on a segment about whistleblowing. I agreed to do it in my role as president of the WAG. The ABC ran a series of promos a few days ahead of filming the program which alerted the senior executive of the police service that I was about to let rip again. On the day the program was to go to air I was working in my office. Nobody asked me about the program, although I had no doubt that it was the subject of feverish speculation on the upper floors. As I left work that evening, I said to the superintendent who worked down the corridor from me, 'I'll see you tomorrow.'

As I headed for the lift he called out to me, 'Col, I hear you're appearing on the *7.30 Report* tonight. The deputy commissioner has asked me to find out why you are appearing on the program. Is it about not being promoted?'

I told him it had nothing to do with not being promoted. I didn't expect any more promotions; I knew that my career had gone as far as it could under the current administration. I said, 'Tell the deputy he can tune in at 7.30 p.m. tonight if he really wants to know what I'm going to say.'

That was the end of our conversation. It made me laugh that he had been sitting a few metres from me for the whole day stewing over how to broach the question of what I was going to say on television, only to have to tell the deputy commissioner to watch it for himself.

The program was broadcast as scheduled that evening. I went to work the next morning and as I passed the superintendent's office I bade him a cheerful good morning. He said the same but neither of us mentioned my interview on the *7.30 Report*.

Later on I was at the cafeteria when a sergeant who worked in the deputy commissioner's office told me, 'The board of management met this morning and you were the main topic of conversation.'

For a moment I thought he was joking. He went on, 'The question was raised about what should be done to make you toe the line.' He said there was a long silence before one of the assistant commissioners said, 'The smart thing to do would be to leave him alone. If we were to make a move against him the media would tear us apart.'

***

The assistant commissioner was probably right. However disliked I was by other police, I had the support of the media and the public. I had never forgotten the letters I had received from ordinary Queenslanders after giving evidence at the Fitzgerald Inquiry. I didn't believe that I was untouchable, or that there were not people out there who hated my guts, but I was reasonably confident that my 'notoriety' as a whistleblower afforded me some protection against reprisals.

A few years later I would find out what it felt like to be attacked by the media.

SEVENTEEN

Flying the flag for NAIDOC Week

When I arrived at the Cultural Advisory Unit I genuinely believed that it served a useful purpose. But the longer I was there, the more I realised that it was nothing more than a shop front. My strong view is that under Commissioner O'Sullivan there was no real commitment inside the Queensland Police Service to improving relationships with Indigenous Australians.

Certain individuals, such as assistant commissioners Frank O'Gorman and David Jefferies, were certainly motivated to mend relations and they helped develop programs to facilitate the recruitment of Indigenous police officers.

Assistant Commissioner Errol Walker was another who took practical steps to build bridges between the police and Aboriginal people. While stationed at Townsville and in charge of the far northern region, he initiated a trial program by recruiting two Indigenous police liaison officers, whose role was to liaise between the police service and Indigenous communities. The trial proved so successful that it eventually went state wide.

Others, however, showed no interest at all and resented any visits I made in my capacity as head of the Cultural Advisory Unit. I remember one assistant commissioner telling a colleague of mine, 'Dillon doesn't want to get any ideas about coming into this region while I'm in charge.'

The Queensland Police had changed since the day I joined, when another policeman could openly tell his colleagues that he would refuse to walk on the same side of the street as me, but it hadn't changed enough. An Aboriginal kid like Daniel Yock could still die in the back of a police paddy-wagon. There were still racists in the Queensland Police Service and most of the leadership didn't seem to have a clue about how to improve relations with the Indigenous community.

***

With tensions still running high after the Pinkenba incident and the death of Daniel Yock, a letter was sent out by the police service inviting Aboriginal and Torres Strait Islander leaders to attend a meeting at Police Headquarters in Roma Street. Indigenous groups agreed to the meeting, which was aimed at sorting out issues that had been festering for some time and needed to be resolved before dialogue could be re-established between us.

About thirty Indigenous leaders came to the meeting, which was attended on the police side by around twenty senior officers, including deputy and assistant commissioners, superintendents and inspectors. It was the biggest meeting I had ever seen or attended between police and the Aboriginal and Torres Strait Islander communities. The status and seniority of the Indigenous representatives was a clear indication of the importance they placed on the meeting and the same could also be said of the police. For the first time I sensed a genuine desire on both sides to break the deadlock.

The two leaders who would sit at the table and try to negotiate a way forward couldn't have come from more different worlds. Deputy Commissioner Bill Aldridge was a career police officer who had come from the Victoria Police in the aftermath of the Fitzgerald Inquiry. Across the table from Aldridge was Santa Unmeopa, a man of Torres Strait Islander heritage who had been elected chairperson of the Aboriginal and Torres Strait Islander Commission's southeast Queensland Regional Council. Unmeopa was a born leader who had spent his adult life fighting for social justice for Indigenous Australians. When it came to a political stoush over Indigenous issues, Unmeopa was a force to be reckoned with.

I had attended quite a few similar meetings as inspector in charge of the Cultural Advisory Unit and I had come to expect heated argument from both sides. The meetings called for diplomacy and sensitivity—neither of which were in abundant supply in the higher reaches of the Queensland Police Service. In my experience the only two men with the tact and authority to chair orderly meetings were Frank O'Gorman and David Jefferies.

On this occasion the early signs were not good. Aldridge seemed uncomfortable in his role as chair while the Indigenous representatives gave the impression that they did not expect the meeting to achieve anything. I was already beginning to think that the meeting was going to be a waste of time when Santa Unmeopa stood up and spoke directly to Aldridge. He said, 'We, the Aboriginal and Torres Strait Islander community of Brisbane, are well aware of the fact that our brother here, Col Dillon, one of your own police officers, is not treated to or afforded the respect and dignity that he deserves. I want to make it quite clear to you right now that if you wish to have any future dialogue with us you will certainly have to change your attitude and also the treatment that is dished out to him. Col is one of us and he is our man and if you wish to have any communication with our community at all then you come through Col.'

After saying those few words, Unmeopa looked to his right and left and signalled to the Indigenous people who had accompanied him that the meeting was over and it was time for them to withdraw.

Aldridge didn't know what had hit him. He sat there dumbstruck as the Indigenous representatives got up and left.

Unmeopa's statement caught me completely by surprise. On a practical level, I was disappointed that the meeting had collapsed because I knew that unless we could start talking again there would be no solution to the stand-off between the police and Indigenous people. But on a personal level, Unmeopa's expression of solidarity with me represented the first time in my career as a police officer that I had felt accepted by my own community. I had become used to being seen by many Aboriginal people as a sell-out who had joined the ranks of the enemy. It never occurred to them that I wasn't truly accepted by the 'enemy' either. As hard as I had tried to bring both sides together, I often felt that I belonged to neither.

When Aldridge got over his initial shock he turned to me and said, 'Col, what's going on—why are your people walking out? Is there anything you can do to get them to stay, at least until we finish the meeting?'

I knew then that to Aldridge, having the meeting was more important than whether or not it actually achieved anything. He couldn't guide both parties towards a solution because he didn't understand what the problems were. As chair, he was simply out of his depth.

I said, 'No, there isn't anything I can do or say that will make them stay. I believe they came in good faith but they didn't like what they saw in this room.'

When he asked what I meant, I said that they couldn't fail to have picked up on the 'them and us' attitude coming from the police side. I told him that in New South Wales the commissioner of police put aside two full days a year to meet with Indigenous leaders and elders from all over the state, and that the meetings were always held at a neutral venue; whereas up here, we expected to hammer out a deal over a couple of hours at Police Headquarters.

Aldridge looked far from pleased, as if he half suspected the walk-out was my idea. He said, 'Col, I'm relying on you to try and set up another meeting because we can't keep on going the way we are.'

I replied, 'OK, but I'll tell you upfront that won't be easy because once they've been offended it's going to take some time for me to persuade them to return for any further discussions.'

We had botched one chance at reconciliation but it wouldn't be long before an opportunity arrived for Aldridge to redeem himself. Meanwhile the police and the Aboriginal and Torres Strait Islander community remained poles apart. Continual pressure was put on me to encourage Indigenous leaders to return to the table but nothing would convince them to come back until they could see some evidence on the police side of a real change of heart.

***

Every year the National Aborigines and Islanders Day Observance Committee (NAIDOC) hosts celebrations across the nation starting in the first week of July and running for a week. The events are designed to showcase the history, culture and social achievements of Aboriginal and Torres Strait Islander people. One of the highlights of NAIDOC Week is a national ball, which is held in a different capital city each year and caters to people from all walks of life from both Indigenous and non-Indigenous societies.

NAIDOC was established in 1957 and could be a great force for reconciliation but many white Australians have never heard of it. The media show no interest and would rather perpetuate negative stereotypes of Aboriginal people as drunkards and bludgers than highlight the rich Aboriginal culture on display during NAIDOC Week.

CODE OF SILENCE

NAIDOC family fun day is held every year in Musgrave Park in South Brisbane, a traditional meeting place for Aboriginal peoples long before Europeans came to Australia. It is a joyous occasion and is always well attended by non-Indigenous families and members of ethnic communities who have always been strong supporters of my people's quest for social justice and reconciliation. The Musgrave Park family day is absolutely drug and alcohol free and this rule is strictly enforced by responsible members of the Aboriginal and Torres Strait Islander communities.

I have attended the celebrations in Musgrave Park many times. Every year I am dismayed by the number of police on display, often dressed in riot gear and with a couple of paddy-wagons at the ready. The police always stand on a hill overlooking the park; I have never seen them mingle with people attending the festivities to try to rebuild trust. In Queensland it always seems to be 'them' and 'us'.

On my visits to Western Australia I often saw the Aboriginal flag flying alongside the Australian flag on government buildings. The first time I saw this it made my heart swell with pride and gave me hope that one day there could be reconciliation between our cultures.

Around April 1993 it occurred to me to make some inquiries within my own department to see whether or not the police hierarchy would be receptive to the idea of flying the Aboriginal and Torres Strait Islander flag from Police Headquarters during NAIDOC Week. If I could make it happen I thought it would be seen by Aboriginal people as a sign of goodwill and might help to end the stand-off between the police service and the Indigenous community.

I knew that any request put forward by me to have the Aboriginal flag hoisted from Police Headquarters would be met with strong resistance, but little did I know how strong.

***

FLYING THE FLAG FOR NAIDOC WEEK

Before submitting a written proposal I made inquiries with the protocols officer at the Queensland Parliament, who confirmed that the Aboriginal flag was recognised and deemed to be an official flag within the Commonwealth of Australia and furthermore that there was no law against it being flown from federal or state buildings.

My office, the Cultural Advisory Unit, came under the command of Assistant Commissioner Ron McGibbon, so the paperwork would eventually end up on McGibbon's desk and he would be the one to make the decision.

It was McGibbon who had given me feedback after my unsuccessful bid for promotion to inspector and who had told me, 'You need a lot more development before you think about applying for your next promotion.' I couldn't see McGibbon falling over himself to let me have my way in hoisting the Aboriginal flag over Police Headquarters during NAIDOC Week.

Before being transferred back to Brisbane to take charge of Operations Support Command, McGibbon had been stationed in Toowoomba in charge of the Southern Police Region. When I heard that he was returning to Brisbane and would have control over the Cultural Affairs Unit, I thought it might be in my interest to check out what he was like as a boss. I phoned a friend of mine, a fellow inspector who had worked under McGibbon in Toowoomba. Dave Fitch and I had worked together as young constables at Innisfail back in the 1960s. He was an honest, forthright and very competent police officer.

After giving me an objective appraisal of McGibbon's leadership, Dave added a word of warning: McGibbon had a hot temper and whenever he was about to blow he would grab the band of his wristwatch before ripping it from his wrist and smashing it down on his desk.

I knew that McGibbon would not make it easy for me but at the same time I felt strongly that if McGibbon gave me the nod to hoist the Aboriginal flag over Roma Street, that gesture could transform relations between Indigenous people and the police.

It was around this time that a future police commissioner, Bob Atkinson, received another quick promotion from superintendent to chief superintendent and was appointed as staff officer to McGibbon. His rapid rise left no one in any doubt that Atkinson was being groomed for bigger things. The partnership between McGibbon and his staff officer, Bob Atkinson, was so close that in conversations around the office, people would routinely refer to McGibbon as 'Dad' and Bob as his 'Son'.

I made an appointment to meet McGibbon, having already been tipped off by another mate, Tony, that McGibbon would not see me alone but would insist on having another senior officer present. I told Tony that I didn't think McGibbon would bother in this case, since there was no disciplinary element involved. 'Just watch,' said Tony.

I arrived at McGibbon's office and was met by his personal assistant, who took me in. McGibbon was sitting at his desk with another senior officer in the room: it was no other than my 'old friend' Gronow (by now he had been promoted to superintendent). I thought Gronow must have had his own appointment with McGibbon and assumed he was about to leave.

McGibbon's first words to me as I entered his office were, 'Col, when you walk through that door I only want you to bring me solutions, not problems.'

I thought to myself that it should have been the other way around: McGibbon was one of the seven top executive officers in the police service and if I had any problems, surely I should have felt at ease in coming to him for advice.

Gronow sat back in his chair and didn't seem in any hurry to leave. I glanced at McGibbon to let him know that I thought we had a meeting, just him and me. McGibbon caught my meaning at once and said, 'I've asked Superintendent Gronow to sit in on our meeting. I never meet with my inspectors unless I have another senior officer present.'

Tony's advice had been spot-on.

Our conversation didn't last long. My written request to fly the Aboriginal flag over Police Headquarters had been on his desk for at least a fortnight but McGibbon still hadn't made up his mind. As I got up to leave, McGibbon repeated his earlier remark, 'Don't forget, Col, only bring me solutions, not problems.'

NAIDOC Week wasn't far off and I was still waiting for McGibbon to make a decision. As I left my office and walked through the atrium I saw Bob Atkinson walking towards me. Bob had a sense of humour as dry as the Simpson Desert but his solemn demeanour could lead people to believe that he was totally humourless. He had a rather peculiar habit of constantly pinching the bridge of his nose between his thumb and forefinger, giving the impression of a man who was carrying the troubles of the world on his shoulders. 'Col,' he said, 'I've been asked to tell you that your proposal is coming along fine.'

I stared at him for a few moments, wondering if he was pulling my leg. 'Bob,' I said, 'that's bullshit and you know it. I gave the assistant commissioner a full report a couple of weeks ago and since then I haven't heard a word. All it needs is a simple yes or no. The event in question is almost here and if the answer to my request is yes then I'm going to have to send out a stack of invitations to community members.'

Bob raised both hands apologetically. He could see that I was running out of patience. 'Leave the matter with me, Col,' he said. 'I'll chase it up right away.'

Bob was as good as his word. The telephone rang and McGibbon's personal assistant told me that an appointment had been scheduled for me to meet McGibbon on

Wednesday, 22 May 1993 at 9.30 a.m. I was to attend with my supervisor. Strictly speaking that ought to have been Superintendent Gronow, but by some process I didn't understand I found myself reporting to a relatively junior public servant—a situation I didn't like but couldn't do much about, although it was a blatant breach of police protocol.

On the Wednesday I started work at 7 a.m. At 9.30 I went with my public servant supervisor to Assistant Commissioner McGibbon's office. (The following record of the meeting comes from my official police diary.)

The three of us began to discuss the question of whether or not it was possible to fly the Aboriginal flag from Police Headquarters during NAIDOC Week. Three flags—the Commonwealth flag, the Queensland flag and the police flag—normally flew over Police Headquarters. The problem, McGibbon said, was deciding which of the three should be taken down to make way for the Aboriginal flag.

I said it didn't seem much of a problem since we were only talking about flying the Aboriginal flag for a week during the NAIDOC celebrations.

'The difficulty I have is in taking down the police flag,' said McGibbon. 'I have six thousand police out there; four thousand may not care but the other two thousand may care.'

I said, 'A precedent was set by the police service only last year in Townsville when the Aboriginal flag was flown from the Regional Headquarters and was favourably received by all, particularly the Indigenous community.'

McGibbon said, 'The population of Townsville is less than 200,000. There are two million people in Brisbane. That makes a big difference.'

McGibbon's body language and the tenor of his voice made it perfectly clear that he wasn't going to agree to my request. 'I don't want racism brought into this,' he said,

FLYING THE FLAG FOR NAIDOC WEEK

although I hadn't mentioned racism. 'I don't want any problems, I'm asking you for solutions. Give me something I can go to the commissioner with.'

'Look,' I said, 'my report was compiled in good faith and I considered it to be a positive initiative in light of the precedent set in Townsville.'

I had the feeling that McGibbon simply did not understand the issue. He was talking about it purely in terms of not offending the police. He didn't seem to have the faintest idea about the history of conflict between Aboriginal people and the authorities. I tried to explain why so many Aboriginal people didn't trust the police, but before I could finish what I was saying McGibbon cut me off. 'Leave racism out of this,' he snapped. 'Forget about racism.'

He was the one fixated on the word 'racism', not me.

I said, 'No other group has such a history of conflict with the police as the Aboriginal race.'

'I disagree and I'll come back to that later,' said McGibbon. 'My point is that it is racist to allow one particular group to fly their flag from Police Headquarters. I must confess I don't really know the significance of NAIDOC Week and that's why I asked you and your supervisor to come and brief me on the matter. I'll have to go to the commissioner with this and I'll need all the information I can get.'

I explained what NAIDOC Week was and why it was important to the Indigenous community, but McGibbon was preoccupied with what the police would think.

'My problem is that I'm going to have two thousand police up in arms about the flag,' he said. 'What am I going to say to them?'

'If that's the way you see it,' I said, 'then it's up to you to try and change the attitude of those in the service with racist views and if you find that's not possible then show them the door. Let them know that racism won't be tolerated in the police service.'

'There must be other options,' said McGibbon. 'Perhaps a display of artefacts in the vestibule. We could use you for a role model. Let the people see the rank you have been promoted to.'

I took real offence at that. I said, 'Would that be in addition to raising the flag? There's no way in the in the world I'll let you use me as some object of curiosity for people to stare at.'

As I said it I noticed McGibbon slip his fingers under the band of his wristwatch. In a flash he ripped it off and threw it down on his desk in front of me. I thought, 'I'm not having this.' The very instant his watch hit the desk I also removed mine and slammed it on his desk. We sat there glaring at each other over our watches.

McGibbon dismissed my supervisor and yelled for Chief Superintendent Bob Atkinson, who was in the office across the corridor. 'Bob,' he shouted, 'come in here and take notes of our conversation.'

Bob dutifully came rushing into his office and started writing before he'd even sat down.

I looked at Bob and said, 'Bob, this is bullshit. Nobody needs to take notes. Let's just talk this matter out and maybe I can walk out of this office with a decision.'

McGibbon snapped back, 'Bob, keep taking notes.'

I said to McGibbon, 'If you're looking for a solution, I have one: just tear up my bloody report.'

'Leave emotions out of this,' said McGibbon.

'I'm not being emotional,' I said. 'You're looking for solutions and I've just given you one. But I'm telling you, this is a golden opportunity for you to do something that will really make a difference. If you agree to raise the Aboriginal flag over Police Headquarters it will sheet home the message loud and clear to those in the service with a racist mentality that those sort of attitudes will not be condoned by the commissioner.'

There was a long silence. Then McGibbon made a statement that took me completely by surprise. He said,

FLYING THE FLAG FOR NAIDOC WEEK

'I suppose all we have ever done until now is pay lip service to multiculturalism.'

'You're spot on,' I said. 'That is the first acknowledgement I have ever heard at this level that lip service is all this service gives to Indigenous and multicultural issues.'

For a moment I thought the argument was over and that McGibbon was going to agree to fly the Aboriginal flag over Roma Street. In a calmer voice he asked me, 'How many flag poles are there in front of Police Headquarters?'

I told him there were three and that I understood the Australian flag and the Queensland flag would keep flying. That left the police flag, which could be set aside for a week so that the Aboriginal flag could be flown.

McGibbon flatly refused and said no way.

That appeared to be the end of it. For all his talk about multiculturalism, it was obvious that McGibbon wasn't going to budge. I wondered where that left me. I had another three years before I would be eligible for voluntary retirement but I wasn't sure I wanted to keep working in a police service where such attitudes still prevailed.

I had one more shot in my locker. With Bob still obediently taking notes of the conversation, I said to McGibbon, 'A senior executive officer in the Queensland Police Service recently told the audience at a public meeting that it was hard to recruit Indigenous people to the service because of their low intellect.'

There was a deafening silence. I noticed that Bob had stopped writing. He sat with pen poised over his pad looking to McGibbon for direction, but McGibbon was too startled to speak. After what he had just admitted about the police service only paying lip service to multiculturalism, what could he say?

A trusted friend of mine was at the meeting where the insulting comment was made. He told me that the senior officer repeated the same comment on two more occasions

185

during the meeting, and that many of those in the audience were flabbergasted to hear those words. To me, it was no surprise at all, because I had heard this person say the very same thing at another forum.

I want to make it clear that not all police were racist and that there were many good police and some exceptional officers who worked tirelessly to improve relations with Indigenous people by treating them with respect and dignity. But I had experienced enough racism during my career to know that it existed in all ranks of the police, from the executive to the lowliest constable.

Nothing else was said. As I stood up to leave McGibbon's office, I glanced at Bob, who looked as though he had been frozen in time. I presumed he had a lot more writing to do after I left.

The next day I learnt that Assistant Commissioner McGibbon had been treated by the service to an overseas trip and had already left for England. NAIDOC Week would start soon. With McGibbon away, I decided to make one last attempt to resolve the issue of the flag.

I phoned the office of Deputy Commissioner Bill Aldridge and spoke to his staff officer, Inspector Bob Summers, a genuinely nice man who treated everyone decently. I said, 'Bob, what are my chances of seeing the deputy? I only need five minutes with him.'

Bob replied, 'Not a problem, Col. You can come around straight away and see him if you like.'

That's how obliging Bob was, that he was prepared to squeeze you in to see the deputy commissioner at a moment's notice despite his busy schedule.

I told Bob I was on my way.

Aldridge walked into the office and gave me a warm greeting. 'Hello, Col,' he said. 'What can I do for you?'

I said, 'Thanks for seeing me at such short notice. I'll be as brief as I can. NAIDOC Week is a very significant event

FLYING THE FLAG FOR NAIDOC WEEK

for Indigenous people all over Australia. The Aboriginal and Torres Strait Islander communities join together in hosting cultural activities in every major city around the nation. I'm here to ask if you would consent to me making arrangements to have the Aboriginal flag fly from Police Headquarters for the duration of NAIDOC Week, which is from 5 to 10 July.'

Without a second's hesitation Aldridge said, 'Col, I think that's a tremendous idea. You make the necessary arrangements and let me know on the day if you want me to turn out in full uniform. I want to be sure that I don't breach any protocols with your people.'

I thanked him and told him it was much appreciated.

I have to admit that his decisiveness amazed me. Whether it signalled a real change of heart by Aldridge I don't know. He would certainly have known that in terms of goodwill he was deeply in deficit to my people and that this was an opportunity for him to redeem himself by extending an olive branch on behalf of the police service.

When all was said and done it was a simple gesture that cost the police service nothing but it would prove to be a ground-breaking decision that paved the way for a better relationship between Indigenous people and the police.

I left Aldridge's office feeling elated. But there was more to the story. The next day I asked our building services coordinator, Neil Henderson, to contact the Premier's department to find out what the protocols were with respect to the flying of flags—and in particular the Aboriginal flag—from state government buildings. Neil floored me by saying he had already seen correspondence from the Premier's department giving approval for the Aboriginal flag to be flown from Police Headquarters during NAIDOC Week.

I couldn't believe what I was hearing. Although I knew that the flying of flags was part of his area of responsibility, I felt that in this instance he had to be mistaken. If what Neil was telling me was true then why had I never seen the

CODE OF SILENCE

Aboriginal flag flying over Roma Street? Why had there never been a formal ceremony? I asked Neil if it would be possible to obtain a copy of the correspondence. Later he contacted me to say he had found it. I hurried round to his office. There it was in black and white on a letterhead from the Premier's department, Executive Building, 100 George Street, Brisbane. It was addressed to the commissioner of police, Mr J. O'Sullivan, and stated:

> In response to previous requests for permission to fly the Aboriginal flag on State Government buildings during NAIDOC Week, in 1992 Cabinet adopted the following policy:
>
> During NAIDOC Week each year, the Aboriginal flag may be flown on or adjacent to Queensland Government buildings and establishments in combination with the Australian and Queensland Flags. However, where there are fewer than three flagpoles, it should not replace either of these flags.
>
> The Premier has decided, in response to a number of requests, that the present policy be upgraded during NAIDOC Week 1993 to reflect the special significance and importance of the International Year for the World's Indigenous People. The policy for NAIDOC Week 1993 from 5th–10th July 1993 will be:
>
> Where there are only two flagpoles, that the Australian Flag may be accompanied by either the Aboriginal or Torres Strait Islander Flag. In the case of three or more flagpoles, that the Aboriginal Flag or the Torres Strait Islander Flag be flown after the Australian and the Queensland Flag.
>
> The Premier believes that the flying of Indigenous flags during NAIDOC Week 1993 will assist the goal of achieving greater recognition of Aboriginal and Torres

> Strait Islander culture during the International Year for the World's Indigenous People.
>
> Could you please ensure that officers of your Department responsible for the flying of flags on Queensland Government buildings are aware of the NAIDOC Week policy?

I asked Neil whether he had ever received a directive from O'Sullivan's office about whether the Aboriginal flag was to be flown or not. Neil said that he hadn't. The police service didn't even own an Aboriginal flag and I had to make urgent inquiries so that I could buy one in time for the start of NAIDOC Week.

It was going to be a historic occasion for the Aboriginal community and I had no doubt about who should have the honour of hoisting the flag: 'Uncle' Neville Bonner, AO, a former Liberal senator and the first Aboriginal person ever to be elected to parliament.

When NAIDOC Week arrived, O'Sullivan was away and the deputy commissioner stood in for him. The role of master of ceremonies was performed by none other than Assistant Commissioner Ron McGibbon.

Seeing that flag rippling in the breeze was one of the proudest moments of my career. Only McGibbon and I knew the story behind it.

EIGHTEEN

Would things ever change?

I was spending a few weeks' holiday in my home town of Caloundra on Brisbane's near north coast when I received a telephone call from Senator John Herron, the federal Minister for Aboriginal and Torres Strait Islander Affairs. Senator Herron asked if we could meet as he had a proposition to put to me about accepting a position on the Aboriginal and Torres Strait Islander Commission (ATSIC).

Senator Herron drove to Caloundra to discuss the idea. As the minister, he was empowered to appoint two commissioners to the board of ATSIC. He was offering one those positions to me. He asked me to give the matter careful consideration because if I accepted the appointment it would be for a period of three years. I was 52 years old and had been a police officer for 32 years. In three more years I would be able to take voluntary retirement, but I wasn't sure I would last that long. I was sure that O'Sullivan and McGibbon were determined to get rid of me.

I had always expected to end my working life in the police service, but the battles had left me exhausted. Accepting Senator Herron's offer meant that I would not have to return to my job in the police. If I did return, it would have to be on my own terms, not O'Sullivan's. I decided to accept the ATSIC appointment.

Joining ATSIC, I thought, would give me the chance to become involved in the lives of my own people. As long as men like O'Sullivan and McGibbon were in charge, I felt that the Queensland Police Service would never regard me as anything other than the token Aboriginal inspector.

This impression had been hammered home by something that happened a year or so earlier, during a two-day function hosted by members of the state's Indigenous Coordinating Council and the government-appointed Aboriginal and Torres Strait Islander Advisory Board. The function was held at the Parliamentary Annex in George Street, Brisbane.

One of the speakers was the new member for Oxley, Pauline Hanson, who was making a name for herself as a rabble-rouser and who had been mouthing off about Aboriginal people on welfare. Oxley had quite a number of Indigenous constituents and this was an opportunity for Hanson to address the Aboriginal delegates and either confirm or deny the allegations that she was racist not only towards Indigenous Australians but also towards people of ethnic origins.

By all accounts Ms Hanson ended up not delivering her speech and she left when several of the Indigenous female elders in the room took offence at some comments she had made.

On the second day McGibbon was scheduled to attend the function to address the two Indigenous organisations on behalf of the police service. After Hanson's reception the previous day, it was a fair bet that he would face a bit of hostility.

WOULD THINGS EVER CHANGE?

I happened to be on leave at the time the function took place. There was no need for me to be there as there were several highly capable and well-respected officers in the Cultural Affairs Unit, any of whom could have accompanied McGibbon to the Parliamentary Annex.

Senior Sergeant Matt Wilson was one whom I considered to be a real asset to the police service. Matt phoned me at home and said he had instructions from McGibbon to come and see me urgently. Matt drove to my house and told me what had happened the day before when Pauline Hanson had been chased from the premises by some of the Indigenous women she had upset. Matt said 'Dad', aka McGibbon, must have received the worst possible feedback about what had transpired at the annex and that he was beside himself at the prospect of having to make a speech the following day.

Respectful as always, Matt said, 'Inspector, I have explicit instructions from Dad to get a message to you no matter what that he needs you in his office at eight o'clock sharp tomorrow morning to accompany him to the Parliamentary Annex. I tried telling him that you were on leave and that you could be anywhere. He told me, "I don't care where he is. Just make sure you find him and tell him to be in my office at 8 a.m. tomorrow. We can credit him a day's leave some other time."'

Matt finished by saying, 'Inspector, if you tell me you're not going to front tomorrow I'll have to fall on my sword rather than go back and give him the bad news.'

'No need for that, Matt,' I said. 'Tell Dad I'll be in his office tomorrow at 8 a.m. as requested.'

I arrived at McGibbon's office at the nominated time. There was no exchange of pleasantries and McGibbon did not apologise for pulling me away from my holidays. He said 'We have to go down to the Parliamentary Annex where I am to speak to the Indigenous conference. You'll do the driving.'

To my surprise, we were going alone: there was no senior officer to give McGibbon moral support. There would just be the two of us in the car. I drove out of the underground car park and swung onto North Quay. As we headed for Parliament House I turned to McGibbon and said, 'This is our opportunity for a man to man conversation.'

I waited for him to slap me down but he looked too startled to say a word.

I went on, 'I'm talking about Col Dillon and Ron McGibbon, not Inspector Dillon and Assistant Commissioner McGibbon.'

After some hesitation McGibbon said, 'OK.'

I said, 'You've pulled me off my holidays and away from my family, which I'm not too happy about, but I accept that it's your prerogative. What really sticks in my craw is that you've got the jitterbugs about fronting the Indigenous conference after the reception Pauline Hanson got yesterday and you think that by having me there beside you, you'll be saved from getting the treatment she did. Well, you could be in for a surprise. If they decide to take you on and tell you a few home truths about the police service, don't expect them to go easy out of courtesy to me.'

I parked our unmarked vehicle and we started walking. As we approached the Parliamentary Annex I asked McGibbon if he was wearing his watch.

He said, 'Yes.'

I said, 'I suggest you take the bloody thing off and put it in your pocket in case anyone upsets you and you're tempted to take it off and smash it on the lectern. This is certainly not the place for anything like that.'

I couldn't believe my eyes when I saw him remove his watch and put it in his pocket.

When we entered the annex I was warmly greeted by my people, as I knew I would be. They were fiercely proud of the fact that one of their own had made it into the upper echelons of the police service. After having felt for so long like an outcast, it was a wonderful feeling for me to know that I was accepted by my people as well as by my brothers and sisters from the Torres Strait Islands. McGibbon, too, was given a courteous welcome. There was no sign of the hostility he had expected and it was clear that the audience passionately hoped for better relations between their communities and the police.

I could see Dad growing in confidence as he finished his speech. Over morning tea we engaged in friendly and positive conversation with the delegates. As we bid farewell, he strode from the annex with the swagger of a four-star general after a victorious battle.

***

My leave of absence from the police service became official on 6 December 1996 when Senator Herron announced that I had been appointed as a non-elected commissioner to the Aboriginal and Torres Strait Islander Commission. My appointment was well received both inside and outside the Indigenous community and I received a flood of congratulatory phone calls and letters.

Before taking up Senator Herron's offer of a place on the ATSIC board, I had asked him to obtain in writing a commitment from Commissioner O'Sullivan that at the end of my three-year term with ATSIC I would be able to see out my career with the Queensland Police Service. Senator Herron was well aware of my difficult relationship with O'Sullivan and he was true to his word in obtaining O'Sullivan's agreement.

I knew that joining the ATSIC board would throw me straight into the world of hard politics. I didn't consider myself a politician, although as president of the Whistleblowers Action Group I had learnt to mix it with a few political hardheads.

There were only two government appointees to the board: the appointed chairperson, Gatjil Djerrkura, and me.

The other members were elected through a voting process conducted by the Australian Electoral Commission. I was worried that those who had been voted onto the board would be suspicious of Gatjil and myself and consider us to be 'yes men' for the government. Furthermore, although I had leave of absence for three years, I still retained my full powers as a police officer. I wondered what some of my colleagues would think of having a 'copper' serving with them on the board.

It didn't take long for me to find out the answer to that question. Word quickly spread that I was a 'plant' who had been appointed by the minister to report on any inappropriate behaviour by my fellow commissioners. The rumour was absolute rubbish but it caused me a good deal of damage in the early days.

The ATSIC board consisted of nineteen commissioners drawn from all states and territories. Each commissioner was allocated a portfolio in keeping with his or her expertise and talents. As a career police officer with long experience of the justice system, I was given the job of watching over the implementation of recommendations arising out of the 1987 Royal Commission into Aboriginal Deaths in Custody.

As I had been appointed to the board rather than elected, I did not have my own regional constituency and was therefore appointed as the national commissioner, which meant travelling extensively all over Australia. I was on a steep learning curve and struggled to come up with initiatives to help reduce the disproportionate incarceration rates for my people, particularly the young.

My role with ATSIC was a far cry from the token position I had held as officer in charge of the Cultural Advisory Unit. I was now speaking to senior ministers of the Crown at state and federal levels as well as religious and civic leaders in my efforts to repeal some of the punitive legislation that was primarily responsible for the over-incarceration of Indigenous Australians.

WOULD THINGS EVER CHANGE?

I was anxious not to lose touch with the many good people I had known in the police and was regularly invited in my capacity as an ATSIC commissioner to attend the passing out parade for Indigenous recruits inducted into the service.

There were some strong personalities on the ATSIC board and arguments often became heated, especially when they concerned the budget. Wherever a person chose to sit around the table at their first meeting became their place for the next three years. Commissioner Terry O'Shane sat on my immediate right, one place away from Commissioner 'Sugar' Ray Robinson, the deputy chairperson. The two men were by no means friends and were locked in a fierce power struggle. The hostility between Robinson and O'Shane continued throughout my three-year term. Keeping them from each other's throats was an unenviable task that usually fell to me.

During one of their rows, Robinson and O'Shane, both of whom had reputations as useful boxers in their younger days, jumped up out of their chairs and assumed a fighting stance. The remaining commissioners and public servants looked on in horror as they waited for the first punch to be thrown. The chairperson, Gatjil Djerrkura, quickly vacated his seat and shot out of the room, obviously not wanting to become involved in any way in what was about to take place. Nobody made a move to defuse the situation. All eyes turned to me with a look that said, 'Don't just sit there—what are you going to do?'

Since no one else was going to intervene, I stood up and pushed my way between them, grabbing them each by the shirt collar. Over the years I'd been in dozens of similar situations when trying to break up brawls. Both men were so focused on each other that I don't think they realised I was standing between them. I mustered all my strength and shoved both men apart while yelling at them to sit down and behave themselves.

Fortunately this had the desired effect and after a few more recriminations Robinson and O'Shane resumed their seats. There seemed to be a general expectation that I should assume the role of 'in-house policeman' for the duration of my term on the board.

***

On 3 November 1998 the *Courier Mail* published an article by one of its Canberra-based reporters, Helen McCabe, headlined 'Taxpayers fund ATSIC members' loans'.

The article named five ATSIC commissioners, including me, as having obtained cheap housing loans through ATSIC at the Australian taxpayers' expense. The basis of her allegation was an ATSIC annual report that identified the five of us as recipients of taxpayer-funded loans.

McCabe seemed to have done very little research on me before publishing her story. If she had, she would have known that I had never applied for a housing loan (or any other kind of loan) through ATSIC. When I took out a loan to buy a house, it was through the Commonwealth Bank of Australia.

The article was picked up and published in a number of other newspapers on the eastern seaboard. Several newspapers published photographs of me in my full inspector's uniform (there were no photographs of the other four commissioners). Almost the only fact that McCabe got right about me was that I was Australia's most senior ranking Indigenous police officer.

I was in Western Australia when someone contacted me to tell about McCabe's article. I was outraged. Throughout my career I had strived to build a reputation for honesty and integrity and yet here was a reporter, a woman who hadn't even bothered talking to me, telling the world that I was involved in a shonky housing deal.

I rang McCabe the next day and told her that what she had written about me was untrue. She was very belligerent and refused to retract a single word of her article. I challenged her about not having tried to contact me to verify the facts. Her response to that was to say that she had spoken to one of the other commissioners and didn't see any need to talk to me. Before I could ask her another question she hung up on me.

In fact the other four individuals mentioned in her article had taken out housing loans through ATSIC, but all four had done so well before their appointment as commissioners and without knowing that they would one day be appointed to the board of ATSIC. But in my case the allegation was absolutely false. Before hanging up, McCabe had ruled out any chance of an apology, so I had no choice but to sue for defamation.

The case dragged on for months. In the end my lawyers negotiated an out-of-court settlement. I insisted that each of the four newspapers publish an apology on the same page as that on which the original article appeared. The Brisbane *Courier Mail* was the first and Sydney's *Daily Telegraph* the last of the papers to publish the agreed apology. The apology in *The Daily Telegraph* read:

> On 2 November last year *The Daily Telegraph* published an article which said that ATSIC Commissioner Colin Dillon was among board members who had sought and received a home loan from the Aboriginal and Torres Strait Islander Commission.
>
> This claim was false.
>
> *The Daily Telegraph* accepts that Commissioner Dillon, Australia's most senior ranking Indigenous commissioned police officer, has neither applied for, nor received, any loan from ATSIC.
>
> We accept that Commissioner Dillon is a man of unblemished character and integrity who has devoted

much of his professional career to fighting corruption and apologise for any distress or offence to him and his family as a result of the article.

***

As my three years as a commissioner drew to a close in 1999, I began to have second thoughts about returning to the police service. In 2000 I had been awarded an honorary doctorate by the Queensland University of Technology for services to the community. It made me think there could be life for me outside the Queensland Police Service. I still had friends in the service and most of them couldn't wait to get out. I was told that O'Sullivan and McGibbon were dead against my coming back and that they were hoping my appointment with ATSIC would be extended.

Since the Queensland Police Service was in no hurry for me to return, I decided to stand for election to the ATSIC board at the end of my term. I picked up quite a few votes but narrowly missed out on getting elected. I said to Linda, 'It looks like I'm going to have to go back.'

I soon discovered that returning to the QPS wasn't going to be as straightforward as I had imagined. I couldn't just front up one morning after three years' absence and announce, 'I'm back. What position have you got for me?'

I telephoned Ray Beaufoy, the senior public servant in charge of the office of the commissioner, to ask him to arrange a meeting for me with Commissioner O'Sullivan, which I considered the correct protocol. I didn't know Ray very well but I liked him. He suggested we should meet one morning for coffee to chat about my return.

By the time we met, Ray had spoken to O'Sullivan, who he said had been discussing the matter with McGibbon. Ray told me that they had worked something out and told me, 'I'm sure you'll like what they have in store for you.

WOULD THINGS EVER CHANGE?

They haven't exactly told me what it is but you'll find out when you have your meeting with the commissioner.' I came away from my meeting with Ray feeling very optimistic, although I hadn't forgotten what others had told me about O'Sullivan and McGibbon not looking forward to my return.

The day of my meeting with O'Sullivan arrived and I reported to his office on the seventh floor of Police Headquarters. His staff officer took me in. The moment I walked in I realised that my informants had been right. There was going to be no warm welcome from Commissioner O'Sullivan. He cut straight to the chase by telling me that McGibbon (who had been promoted to deputy commissioner) had decided to put me on the major event team that was planning for the Queensland stages of the Olympic torch relay the following year.

I was pleasantly surprised. It sounded like a good project to work on. O'Sullivan didn't ask me what I had been doing during my three years as an ATSIC commissioner, although given his role as the head of the QPS I felt he should at least have arranged for me to address the board of management at some later stage to share my experience of Indigenous affairs at the national level. If the service had been serious about improving its relationship with Indigenous people, it should have jumped at the chance to hear how police in other jurisdictions worked. Maybe, as McGibbon had told me himself, it was just lip service after all.

I was told that I would be reporting to Bob Atkinson, who had now been promoted to the rank of assistant commissioner. I reported to Bob's office to find out where my office was. After the initial small talk, he pinched the bridge of his nose between his thumb and forefinger and said, 'Mate, we're looking for an office for you but in the meantime you can use one across the corridor. The fellow who normally occupies it is on holidays.'

I knew the office he was referring to belonged to his staff officer. When I pointed out that taking another bloke's office wasn't really satisfactory, Bob replied, 'I'm sorry, Col, but we have nowhere else to put you at the moment. I'm working on it but for now you will have to bear with me.'

All the offices on the seventh floor had glass walls. This one was so close to Bob's that the two of us had to stare at each other all day across the corridor.

The Olympic Planning Committee was two floors down on the fifth floor. Inspector Tim Fenlon was in charge. I knew Tim quite well and we had always got on well, but when I went down to say hello it was obvious that Tim didn't know why I was there. It was one of the most humiliating moments of my career. Tim was too much of a gentleman to further embarrass me by asking me the reason for calling at his office. He told me that he and his team had spent the past two years planning for the torch relay and that in a day or two they would be finished.

It was now clear that not only was there no office for me, there was no job either.

I couldn't bear sitting in an office with nothing to do, so I spent the next couple of days roaming Police Headquarters talking to old colleagues.

Finally Ross Dwyer, a qualified barrister who was also the superintendent in charge of the prosecution section, took pity on me and gave me a desk and computer in one of his offices.

The arrival of the Olympic torch was only days away. The QPS was responsible for ensuring that the torch and its runners were safe during the ten-day journey through Queensland. There had been much intelligence gathering for the event and this strongly indicated that the relay runners would be met with hostile demonstrations by Indigenous protesters who wanted to draw international attention to the injustice which the nation's First Peoples continued to suffer at the hands of governments in Australia.

WOULD THINGS EVER CHANGE?

As the torch approached, one of the members of the planning team informed me that McGibbon had given instructions that I was not to be included in the operation until the relay team began its journey in our state. I was then to be provided with a police vehicle and, working alone, I was to precede the torch runners by a couple of kilometres and to negotiate with any Indigenous protesters lying in wait for the relay team to reduce the likelihood of a confrontation.

There was never any job waiting for me in the Major Events Planning Group and nor was there intended to be. It seemed to me that McGibbon was just using me to strong-arm Aboriginal protesters into behaving themselves. I had to hand it to him: he couldn't have chosen a better way to alienate me from my people and to destroy the credibility it had taken me three decades to earn.

I spent a couple of years stewing over the Olympic torch fiasco before I happened to bump into Tim Fenlon in the Queen Street Mall in Brisbane. This was the first time I had seen Tim since the day I walked out of his office squirming with embarrassment after realising there was no job for me. Finally I had the chance to hear the real story. Tim had since left the Queensland Police and was working overseas, so he had no reason not to tell me the truth. He told me that never at any time did either McGibbon or O'Sullivan mention that I would be joining his team on my return from ATSIC. He said that when I came to his office he and the others on his team thought I was simply doing the rounds and had dropped in to say hello. Tim added that if he had been told that I was coming to work with him, I would have been more than welcome.

***

The time had come for me to think seriously about whether it was worth my while remaining in the police. I had notched up 36 years' service and the reality for me was that the door to any further promotion was well and truly closed; I had no chance of advancing beyond where I was. I considered myself very fortunate to have made it to the rank of inspector. Had it not been for Commissioner Newham and his deputy, David Blizzard, I don't believe I would ever have made it beyond sergeant.

When I tried to think of reasons why I should stay in the police service, I couldn't come up with a single one. Linda knew I was worn out by the fighting. As much as she had been against my coming forward to the Commission of Inquiry, Linda knew that without the inquiry there would have been no reform of the police, and that my evidence had played a vital part in the process. Frightened as she was about the consequences for our family, I knew that she was proud of what I had done. But Linda understood that my career in the police was over. I sat down at my computer and resigned by email. After typing my personal and career details into the online form, I read the following question: 'Do you require an exit interview?'

I answered, 'Most definitely not, as I have been a member of the QPS for 36 years and never during that time were my views or opinions sought on any important issues relating to Indigenous affairs as they have impacted on the service.'

All I needed to do after submitting the form was obtain final approval from the commissioner and a clearance from the Crime and Misconduct Commission to ensure there were no outstanding departmental investigations against me. O'Sullivan had gone and Bob Atkinson was the new commissioner, with McGibbon as his deputy. Dad had been overtaken by his son, and that certainly put paid to their once close relationship.

Two weeks' notice was all I was required to give. It was my intention to leave the service as quietly as when I had

WOULD THINGS EVER CHANGE?

first entered the gates at Petrie Terrace Police Training Depot on 11 January 1965 to begin my training as a probationary constable.

Ross Dwyer, the superintendent who had given me an office when nobody else would, approached me discreetly in the days before I was due to leave. 'Col,' he said, 'one of the fellows in my section has told me you have put in your resignation. There are some members here including myself who'd like to come to your send-off when it takes place.'

I said, 'To be honest, Ross, I don't think there will be any send-off for me. Quite frankly, I'll be happy just to slip out the door without any fuss and get on with the next phase of my life.'

'Mate,' he said, 'after all you've done for the QPS in speaking out at the Fitzgerald Inquiry I'm certainly not going to stand by and see you walk out the door without any kind of farewell. Would you at least let me arrange a luncheon for you? All I need is a few names of people you'd feel comfortable with and would like to attend.'

As much as I was reluctant to have a send-off, Ross's kind offer was pretty hard to refuse, so I relented and provided him with a list of about a dozen colleagues with whom I shared a mutual respect.

I will always be grateful to Ross for ensuring that I was able to serve out my last months in the QPS with some respect and dignity. It was the antithesis of the treatment I felt I had received from O'Sullivan, McGibbon and Bob Atkinson.

I walked out the door of headquarters for the last time as a police officer on 6 April 2001 at 5 p.m. sharp. The relief I felt was instantaneous. During my career I had worked with some wonderful people, men and women who every day put their lives on the line to make our society better and safer. These were the people I would miss. But I couldn't look back on my career without thinking about the others who would never forgive me for having given evidence at the Fitzgerald Inquiry, and who had gone out of their way to make things hard for me. Being a policeman was all I had ever wanted to do but the strain of the last fourteen years had been almost more than I could bear. In some ways I felt more like a prisoner set free from a life sentence.

***

Little did I know that a final controversy was waiting for me. I was using up the last of my holiday leave before my employment with the QPS was officially terminated when I received a call from Andrew Carroll, a talkback host on ABC Radio in Brisbane. He wanted me to come on his program to talk about my 36-year career in the police. I liked and trusted Andrew and admired the way he had investigated corruption, so I was happy to accept his invitation.

The interview was done live to air at the ABC studios at Toowong. Most of Andrew's questions were to do with my appearance at the Fitzgerald Inquiry and how this had affected my life. There was nothing really contentious in anything I said until Andrew asked me whether I considered Queensland post-Fitzgerald to be totally clean and free of corruption. I had expected him to ask me something like this and replied that while the government had made considerable progress in terms of implementing the reform process recommended by Fitzgerald, there was still corruption in Queensland. I did not specify where this corruption existed and I did not make any reference to the police, but I did warn that there were signs we were slipping back to the bad old days.

A family member contacted me to say she had heard my interview and thought it had gone quite well. I was pleased by her feedback as I knew she would have been quick to tell me if I had stuffed up. Not long afterwards my mobile phone rang. It was my wife. She was very upset. She said,

WOULD THINGS EVER CHANGE?

'What the hell did you say in your interview? Did you say that the whole of the QPS was riddled with corruption? I've just had two senior police officers from the Professional Standards Unit knocking on our front door demanding to know where you are because they want to question you about what you said in your interview.' One of the officers was Cliff Crawford. He told Linda that the new commissioner, Bob Atkinson, had instructed him to interview me immediately about what I was supposed to have said on ABC Radio.

Linda had been very distressed and ordered them to leave our property immediately and told them that if Bob Atkinson wanted to speak to me then he could do so directly as he knew me personally, which was certainly true.

As Crawford left, he apparently turned and told Linda not to worry as he had just received a message over their police radio that they would not need to see me after all. Naturally there was no apology.

What had happened was that after the interview went to air, the ABC started broadcasting a promo for the evening news in which the lead item was to be a sensational claim by Col Dillon that the QPS was still a hotbed of corruption. I had said no such thing.

Cliff Crawford was a chief superintendent at the time and we had known each other over many years; in fact we had done motor patrols together as young constables back in the early 1970s. I was dismayed that Crawford could have believed me capable of making the sort of reckless comments being attributed to me.

If that wasn't bad enough, the general secretary of the Queensland Police Union of Employees, Merv Bainbridge, was asked by the media to comment on behalf of the membership and he said I should apologise to every decent and hardworking police officer in the state. Merv was another I had known for many years; I found it absolutely incredible that he wouldn't have first contacted me to find out if what people were saying was true.

I immediately telephoned the ABC to find out how they could have put to air claims that were extremely damaging to me and which bore no relation to what I had actually said. I was put through to Andrew Carroll's producer, who was about to leave her office for the day, but she knew nothing about it. I appealed to her to get in touch with Andrew and have him contact me urgently, which he did. Andrew, too, knew nothing about it but promised to make urgent inquiries. He agreed that I had never at any point in the interview suggested that the QPS was still corrupt. (Senior ABC management later came to the same conclusion.) It seemed that transcripts had been sent to the news department and that words and sentences from the interview had been spliced together to give a completely misleading impression of what I had said, and this had formed the basis of the promo.

My next step was to phone Merv Bainbridge to put him straight on what had happened and ask him why he hadn't got in touch with me before sticking the boot in. I was put through to Merv but before I could get a word out, he said, 'Col, as soon as I heard the news the first thing I said to myself was, "Why would Col want to go and bite the hand that feeds him?"' I knew straight away that there was no point talking to him.

Regular promos were still hitting the airwaves with grabs along the lines of 'Retiring police officer and Fitzgerald Inquiry whistleblower Col Dillon claims that the Queensland Police Service is riddled with corruption'. Each time I heard it, it felt like another kick in the guts.

People told me I should have sued the ABC but all I wanted was an apology and correction. On 30 April 2001, more than three weeks after the ABC had trashed what was left of my reputation inside the QPS, I received the following letter:

WOULD THINGS EVER CHANGE?

Dear Mr. Dillon

LETTER OF APOLOGY

During an ABC Radio News broadcast in Brisbane on Thursday, April 6, 2001, we reported that you claimed that corruption was still rife in the Queensland Police Service.

We accept that at no stage before, during, or after your interview with ABC reporter Andrew Carroll, which led to the airing of this report, did you imply or make such a claim.

The ABC wishes to unreservedly apologise to you and your family for airing this report. The ABC accepts the report had no factual basis and may have caused you and your family embarrassment with the wider public and most particularly with members of the Queensland Police Service.

Yours truly
Fiona Crawford
State Editor
News and Current Affairs, Queensland

When demanding an apology from the ABC I stipulated that a copy of the letter be forwarded to the commissioner, Bob Atkinson, and to the secretary of the Queensland Police Union, Merv Bainbridge. Neither of them contacted me afterwards to apologise for having accused me of something without bothering to check whether I was guilty.

Nearly two months later I received in the mail on Queensland Police Service letterhead a short note from Bob Atkinson dated 28 May 2001. It read:

CODE OF SILENCE

Dear Mr. Dillon (Col)

After more than 36 years, your association with this organisation has come to an end.

I would like to express to you my appreciation for your loyalty and dedication to the Queensland Police Service and the people of this State.

On behalf of your colleagues and myself, I extend to you best wishes for the future.

Yours sincerely
R Atkinson.

Two years after I retired, a tip-off to the media revealed that Queensland police officers at a pistol practice range were using cut-outs of male Aboriginal faces for target practice. After all the anger and soul-searching brought about by the Royal Commission into Aboriginal Deaths in Custody, it seemed beyond belief that white men should be honing their skills by firing bullets at black faces. Watching the story on the TV news, I couldn't help wondering whether the police in Queensland would ever change.

NINETEEN

The rise and rise of Detective Tony Murphy

In September 2013 Tony Fitzgerald gave a rare face-to-face interview with a journalist from *The Australian*. In the article the journalist referred to the years between 1987 and 1989 when the inquiry was running and Fitzgerald was the subject of death threats. The police had set up a security post in Fitzgerald's home and at night the grounds were patrolled by armed guards. Sometimes there were police checkpoints in the suburban street in Brisbane's inner west where Fitzgerald and his family lived. His wife and daughters never left the family home without protection. One night, Fitzgerald was warned that he could expect a visit from one of the 'big fish' the inquiry was investigating. According to the person who tipped him off, this visitor was planning to apply 'the frighteners' to force Fitzgerald and his investigators to back off.

Like many Queenslanders I have often wanted to ask Tony Fitzgerald why he cut short the inquiry rather than investigate the trade in illegal drugs. It was disappointing that more effort and resources weren't deployed in pursuing the illicit drug trade in light of the evidence concerning drugs that I provided to the Commission of Inquiry. The other question I would ask Mr Fitzgerald if I ever got the chance is why Tony Murphy was not more vigorously pursued, given the serious allegations against him.

The first time I ever heard Tony Murphy's name mentioned was when I was a junior constable on probation at Roma Street police station. This was in 1965. One night I was the driver of a patrol car with two experienced sergeants when they mentioned Murphy's name in conversation. I clearly recall Murphy being mentioned along with two other detectives, Terry Lewis and Glen Hallahan. (They would become known as the 'rat pack'.) The two sergeants referred to Murphy, Lewis and Hallahan as 'bagmen' for the police commissioner at the time, Frank Bischof. It was the first time I had ever heard the term 'bagmen'. Naturally I was curious but I would not have dared to ask because in those days junior police were not permitted to speak or join in any conversation with their seniors unless invited, and that rarely if ever happened. Junior police were untested and therefore couldn't be trusted by the older members to keep their mouths shut.

Over the years I would hear Murphy's name mentioned, usually in terms of awe if not outright fear. He commanded a lot of respect as a detective in those days when it was standard practice to 'drop a brick' [invent false evidence] in order to ensure a conviction. After the prostitute Shirley Brifman died before she could give evidence against him, there was certainly no shortage of rumours about Tony Murphy having been involved. It was a byword within the police force that Tony Murphy was a man not to be crossed. Before giving evidence to the Fitzgerald Inquiry I had been personally warned by my old mentor, Keith Harris, to beware of Murphy.

THE RISE AND RISE OF DETECTIVE TONY MURPHY

People wondered why he was never dragged before the Commission of Inquiry. In his report, Fitzgerald had quite a bit to say about Tony Murphy's 'chequered career':

> At the time of the National Hotel Royal Commission, he had served in the Consorting Squad of the CIB. He gave evidence at that Royal Commission, and later was transferred to the Licensing Branch, where he served until he was charged with perjury. His trial did not proceed because a vital witness died before the hearing.
>
> Additionally, there was undisputed evidence before this Inquiry by a former s.p. bookmaker that Murphy was paid bribes, and [Basil] Hicks said that Murphy asked him to join in the corruption.
>
> Those allegations may not be true: he has been convicted of nothing and must be presumed to be innocent. However, there were also other matters which affected his reputation and career.
>
> He was a friend and associate of [Jack] Herbert and, with Lewis, named within the Police Force as one of the 'Rat Pack'. He had been a vociferous agitator against [Commissioner Ray] Whitrod and continued to associate with Herbert whilst he was awaiting trial. At the time, Murphy was stationed in Toowoomba and another with whom he was in contact was a notorious s.p. bookmaker.
>
> To say the least, he had a controversial career by the time he and his friend Lewis were sent by Whitrod in late 1975 to their respective postings in Longreach and Charleville from which they successfully set out to cultivate Bjelke-Petersen. The initial proposal was that both would be promoted, Lewis to Assistant Commissioner and Murphy to Superintendent. However, Murphy's rise

had to wait a little while Lewis quickly took the further step which gave him the overall superintendence of the Police Force.

Once Lewis was appointed Commissioner at the end of November 1976 Murphy's rise was swift. He replaced Hicks as head of the CIU [Criminal Intelligence Unit] on 14 January 1977. On 11 August 1977 he was appointed Inspector in charge of the CI Branch. On 31 October 1977 he was promoted to Superintendent over 50 more senior officers and was appointed Detective Superintendent of the CI Branch, exercising supervision of criminal investigations throughout the state.

Thereafter, the controversy continued.

After the Fitzgerald Inquiry, Tony Murphy had such a bad reputation that Jim O'Sullivan was said to have declared that, 'He [Murphy] will never get within a mile of Police Headquarters whilst I'm police commissioner.'

Inspector James Patrick O'Sullivan, as he then was, was the incorruptible Mr Clean to whom Fitzgerald gave the task of choosing a new police hierarchy, so after he became commissioner himself it was no wonder that he didn't want a bar of Murphy. I was more than a little surprised, however, when a senior officer told me one day that he had just seen Tony Murphy enter the main vestibule of Police Headquarters.

At the time I was working in the Professional Standards Unit, so I had more than a passing interest in the career of Tony Murphy. I was keen to verify for myself that it was in fact Murphy whom my colleague had seen and, more importantly, to ascertain who Murphy might be visiting.

I went straight to the head of building security and asked to see the register of visitors. The register was headed 'Police Headquarters—Atrium Entrance—Sheet no.3' and was dated

THE RISE AND RISE OF DETECTIVE TONY MURPHY

9 December 1993. I confirmed that visitor's pass number 165 had been issued against the name of A. Murphy; time in, 11.30 and time out, 12.22. I asked the head of security if he would provide me with a photocopy of the relevant page, which he did. I still have that copy today as proof that Tony Murphy came a lot closer than 'within a mile' of Police Headquarters.

It was puzzling to me that a decade after Murphy had opted for early retirement (under rather dubious circumstances), he was still able to enter Police Headquarters and speak to a very senior officer in the police service.

***

I only met Tony Murphy once, in 1994. Given the warning I received later from Keith Harris, I can only describe the encounter as chilling. It happened not long after I joined the Licensing Branch, where Murphy himself had worked for several years in the late 1960s, and where he was allegedly involved with Jack Herbert in collecting bribes from SP bookmakers.

I was rostered off for a couple of days and needed to go somewhere peaceful to think about what was going on at the Licensing Branch. I knew that I had landed in a hornet's nest. I decided to head for North Stradbroke Island, which was just over an hour away by ferry from the mainland. My plan was to stay at the small tourist getaway of Amity Point, on the island's north-western tip.

The ferry landed at the main township, a place called Dunwich, where Tony Murphy had retired from the police to run the local TAB. The Fitzgerald Report contained some interesting paragraphs about how Murphy came to take over the Dunwich TAB. According to Fitzgerald, Terry Lewis arranged for Sir Edward Houghton Lyons, the chairman of the TAB, to support Murphy's application for the TAB agency on North Stradbroke Island.

Applications for the TAB agency at Dunwich were called on 8 August 1983. The advertisement called for applicants in the 25 to 40 years age group. Murphy, then aged 56 years, applied. Lewis had told Lyons that Murphy wanted the Dunwich agency. Lyons had never met Murphy whom Lewis described as 'a very decent chap'.

The usual method of selection involved an initial choice of some applicants for interview by a committee of TAB executive officers and employees followed by a discussion of their respective merits by Lyons, sometimes the TAB deputy chairman and the TAB general manager. Those discussions usually led to one or two names being put to the board, with a recommendation from the general manager.

Of the 27 applications received for the Dunwich sub-agency, four applicants, including Murphy, were interviewed. Murphy was not the interview committee's first or second choice. However, after Lyons spoke to the general manager, he and Lyons recommended Murphy to the Board and he was subsequently appointed.

Lyons explained to this Inquiry that his decision to recommend Murphy was because he believed that the granting of a TAB agency to Murphy would present a good opportunity to increase the co-operation between the TAB executive and the police in an effort to deal with the SP bookmaking problem.

Between Murphy's appointment and Lyons' resignation from the TAB, Lyons never communicated to Murphy his wish that Murphy should assist the TAB's efforts against SP bookmaking.

In other words, Murphy's appointment to the Dunwich TAB was a joke that perfectly illustrated the extent of corruption in Queensland and how it permeated throughout all levels of government.

After arriving at Dunwich, I waited outside a takeaway seafood shop where I was to meet a friend who had offered to drive me to Amity Point. I kept my distance from the TAB, although I had no reason to fear Murphy since I had never met him and he would not have known who I was (or so I thought). I had been standing outside the fish shop for about ten minutes when I noticed Murphy's large frame emerge from the front door of the TAB. I knew it was Murphy because I had seen his photo in a police journal.

He eyeballed me and said, 'Hi, I'm Tony Murphy. You're young Dillon, aren't you? How's the Licensing Branch going? I served there for a time quite a number of years ago. I think you'll go well in there.'

I found it unnerving to hear Murphy call me by my name. He didn't offer to shake hands. There was no further conversation between us and he went back inside the TAB. It was our first and only meeting. If it had been anyone but Tony Murphy, I probably would have forgotten all about it. But knowing that Murphy knew who I was gave me the jitterbugs. I could only assume that he'd been speaking to one of his mates at the Licensing Branch, and that whoever it was had told him I was causing trouble by arresting people who were paying the police for protection. There was no doubt in my mind that what Murphy was doing was letting me know that he was keeping an eye on me. It wasn't a comforting thought.

After everything that had been said about Tony Murphy at the Commission of Inquiry, I couldn't understand why Fitzgerald chose not to go after him. All we heard from Murphy was a short statement in which he claimed that allegations of corruption against him were 'not only untrue but can be demonstrably proved to be untrue'.

Murphy always had his finger on the trigger when it came to suing for defamation, so the media had become used to tip-toeing around his record. A lawyer once told me that Murphy issued stopper writs that had a lifespan of seven years and would sit in the court registry until he needed to activate them. This rarely happened as Murphy's reputation for violence and intimidation usually ensured that allegations made against him for impropriety were withdrawn by his accusers. When a witness refused to withdraw allegations against Murphy, bad things sometimes happened. Shirley Brifman stuck to her guns and it cost her her life. If Tony Murphy had really felt threatened by the Commission of Inquiry, I sometimes wonder whether Tony Fitzgerald—or I—would still be around today.

TWENTY

'You used to be an inspector in the police force, didn't you?'

In 2002, about a year after I retired from the police, I was offered a job by Frank Rockett, the director of the Department of Aboriginal and Torres Strait Islander Policy. The Beattie Labor Government was trying to clamp down on alcohol-related violence in Indigenous communities and Frank wanted me as an adviser. As I left his office, Frank told me that the minister in charge of Families, Aboriginal and Torres Strait Islander Policy, Disability Services and Seniors, Judy Spence, would want to put out a media release on my appointment to the department.

I said, 'No, Frank. I don't want a media release. I want to be able to do whatever I'm required to do without anyone making a big fuss.'

Frank shook his head. 'Mate,' he said, 'you know what politicians are like. The minister will want to make some mileage out of having you on board.'

A few days later a government media release went out under the headline 'Spence appoints Col Dillon to assist with alcohol reforms'. Part of it read:

> The Minister for Aboriginal and Torres Strait Islander Policy Judy Spence today told State Parliament that former Queensland Police Inspector Dr Col Dillon had been appointed to provide strategic advice on and support for community justice groups to implement tough new alcohol restrictions in Indigenous communities.
>
> 'Dr Dillon was formerly this nation's highest ranked Indigenous police officer and he has extensive government and Indigenous community development experience,' she said.
>
> 'His expertise in the areas of justice, licensing and Indigenous issues and his ability to negotiate in accordance with traditional protocols will be of great benefit to community justice groups.'

Reading it made me furious. I had seen it all before: 'Tell them we're putting Col Dillon in there, that'll shut them up.' It was all politics. Given the sensitive nature of the job, which involved visiting Indigenous communities around the state to research the effects of alcohol, the last thing I needed was publicity—especially publicity reminding everyone that I was (or at least had been) a policeman.

The department—which went under the acronym DATSIP—was a policy unit responsible for advising the Queensland Government on all issues that affected the state's Aboriginal and Torres Strait Islander inhabitants. As well as the main Brisbane office it had regional offices in the major provincial centres.

As usual, there were far more non-Indigenous than Indigenous employees. Several of the Indigenous staff had good tertiary qualifications but hardly any occupied senior positions. Ironically, I saw many Indigenous employees leave DATSIP for other government departments in search of promotion opportunities.

* * *

In early 2005 I was asked to carry out a review of the alcohol management plan on Mornington Island. Alcohol management plans were one of the main recommendations of the Cape York Justice Study undertaken by Judge Tony Fitzgerald. Like many other government initiatives affecting Indigenous communities, they were imposed after very little consultation with the Indigenous people they were going to affect. People I interviewed who had been teetotal all their lives still resented being deprived of their democratic right to decide whether or not their communities should be 'dry'.

I had never visited Mornington Island until I went to work at DATSIP, but I'd heard a lot about it—none of it good. When I was running the Cultural Advisory Unit I had received a phone call from the officer-in-charge at Mornington Island. He told me the place was a hellhole, not just for the men and women posted there as police officers but also for the residents themselves. I will never forget his quavering voice as he started to tell me about the things that went on up there, especially the abuse of kids by people off their faces on alcohol and drugs. He begged me, as head of the CAU, to come up and see the situation for myself so that something could be done to turn the community around. The bloke sounded distraught. I told him I would be happy to come but it would have to be arranged through his district officer, who was stationed at Mt Isa. He said he would do that and get back to me, which he did, only to inform me that he had been told by the district officer that under no circumstances was he to seek any help from me or invite me to visit.

I felt helpless, as though I had let him down, but as his boss had made it clear I wasn't to set foot on the island, there was nothing I could do. I believe the reason for denying me permission to go to Mornington Island was that the commissioner, and probably the minister, were scared that I would call in the media—and if I had found the island half as bad as I had been told, I certainly would have.

I knew that the stories the officer-in-charge had told me were not exaggerations because a few years later Murrandoo Yanner, an Aboriginal activist, told me similar stories of sexual predators roving the streets in packs, waiting for young mothers to become intoxicated with alcohol so that they could move in and assault the children.

I flew to Mornington Island with a staff member from DATSIP. We knew before we arrived that getting reliable information about the alcohol management plan was not going to be easy. Indigenous communities often saw alcohol management plans (AMPs) as just prohibition by another name, and they regarded us as enforcers of prohibition. My being a retired police inspector was probably going to make matters worse. It was only a fact-finding trip but we expected to meet plenty of hostility. What we didn't realise was that our visit would be sabotaged from the start.

Our first appointment after arriving on the island was with the mayor and CEO of Mornington Island Council. My own view was that it was not a good idea to advertise the fact of our visit, but calling on the mayor was a necessary protocol that had to be observed by anyone coming to Mornington Island on government business.

The mayor was far from pleased to see us and she made no effort to hide it. Her first words to me were, 'I was told some people were coming to Mornington to check on the AMPs but I didn't know it was going to be you. You used to be an inspector in the police force, didn't you?'

My heart always sank when I heard that question. To some of my people it was 'once a copper, always a copper'.

'That's right,' I said. 'I retired a couple of years ago.'

'YOU USED TO BE AN INSPECTOR IN THE POLICE FORCE, DIDN'T YOU?'

My reputation as a former police inspector seemed to precede me wherever I went. Usually it was more a hindrance to my work for DATSIP than a help because it made people suspicious and reluctant to talk. Some of them were probably frightened that I'd arrest them if they said too much!

The mayor said, 'I'm providing you with a vehicle and a driver and also another person who can take notes for you.'

The offer of a vehicle was helpful but I didn't really need a driver as I was perfectly capable of driving myself. I certainly had no use for a stranger standing beside me taking notes. I suspected that the reason they were coming along was to ensure that I was taken on a carefully orchestrated guided tour rather than being left to explore the island for myself. Intentionally or not, the presence of the notetaker would discourage people from talking freely to me, since they would know that anything they told me would get back to the mayor. My instinct was to decline the mayor's generous offer but I was a guest on the island and I knew it was impossible for me to say no.

'Thanks,' I said. 'That's very kind of you.'

I knew I was on the right track when, shortly afterwards, the mayor told me that the accommodation we had organised was 'unsuitable' and that she had arranged for us to stay somewhere more convenient. Our new accommodation was a house in the same street as the mayor's—close enough for the mayor to be able to see anyone coming or going. I knew then that our every move on Mornington Island would be closely monitored and the mayor kept well informed of everywhere we went and everyone we spoke to.

We had only been on the island a couple of hours and already our fact-finding visit was starting to look like an exercise in futility. Rather than give up, I excused my driver and his assistant and explained as tactfully as I could that I wanted to hire a vehicle from the council's engineer. The driver wasn't happy about it but he reluctantly agreed.

Even so, I couldn't shake him off and he insisted on following us in case we needed help in communicating with the inhabitants, some of whom (he assured me) would be reluctant to talk to us.

At around 5 p.m. I suggested we call it a day. Once we were alone, I told my colleague that we would wait until the council-run canteen had closed and then make a patrol of the streets at midnight to see for ourselves just how things really were. We already knew that many of the inhabitants drank at the hotel until intoxicated, after which they would continue their binge by drinking 'home brew'. The combination of licensed drinking and home brew fuelled anti-social behaviour that was stretching the island's very limited police resources to the limit and making it virtually impossible for the police to tackle more heinous issues such as vicious assaults; child neglect and molestation; and the trafficking of illicit drugs from the mainland.

Just after midnight my colleague and I set off in our hired vehicle along the island's main road, Lardil Street. What we saw that night were some of the most shocking and heart-wrenching scenes I had witnessed in my life—things I had not seen in nearly four decades of policing.

Lardil Street is roughly 2 kilometres long and built up on both sides. Almost every house we passed was so overcrowded that the occupants were spilling into the street. Everywhere we looked, people were fighting, screaming and shouting. The noise alone would have made sleep impossible. We saw women sprawled on the ground, paralytically drunk; others fighting and brawling with each another, fighting with their men, falling over in the road and incapable of getting back on their feet.

What upset me most were the children wandering the street. We counted 30, perhaps more, ranging from little toddlers up to teenagers. Some of the little ones were wearing nappies and there was no telling how long they had been wearing them or when they would have been last changed. Some were naked from the waist down; some had no upper garments; most looked dirty and undernourished.

Some were obviously being cared for by older siblings; we saw them huddled under the bright streetlights that lined Lardil Street, presumably because that was where they felt safest. Even from the car we could see their dripping noses and the discharge running down their little bare chests.

The only thing I could compare with what I saw that night on Mornington Island was television pictures of African famines and war zones.

As we drove slowly along Lardil Street we could see the predators riding their bikes backward and forwards and doing 'wheelies', no doubt hoping to impress and attract some of the less cautious children.

We made no attempt to approach the children; there were only two of us and there was nothing we could do. The question was where were the people from the Department of Community Services who had the statutory responsibility of protecting these children from neglect, harm and abuse?

The answer to that question was that Mornington Island was serviced from government offices in Mt Isa and Brisbane but only on a fly-in, fly-out basis. The people from DOCS would arrive early in the morning, walk around the streets for a couple of hours and then be on the plane by mid-afternoon to return to the mainland. They never stayed overnight on Mornington Island because the Department of Community Services insisted it was not safe, so they never saw how terrible it was after dark. The same went for government ministers, most of whom would arrive mid-morning accompanied by their advisors to be met by the mayor, who would treat them to morning tea and introduce them to some hand-picked residents. After morning tea they would be taken on a picturesque tour of the island before being shown around the hospital, the school and perhaps the old people's home. They would never meet the victims of alcohol and drug-fuelled violence, the battered wives and mothers, the children who spent the night huddled under streetlights so they would be safe from sexual predators.

After driving around for an hour or so, my colleague and I returned to our accommodation. We got up early, had breakfast and waited for our two escorts, i.e. our driver and note-taker from the previous day. We had a full day's work ahead of us and were keen to get started. At around 9.30 a.m. my mobile phone rang and a woman who did not identify herself informed me brusquely that our driver would not be seeing us today. I told my colleague that we might as well drive down to where our note-taker lived to find out what the story was.

I was about to turn into her street when I noticed three police vehicles parked outside her place and officers walking through her yard. One of the police had his police dog on a leash and was heading towards the back of the house. I put two and two together and told my colleague that the chances were we were not only going to be without our driver but without our note-taker as well.

We pulled in further up the road and watched what was going on. After a while I saw one of the police officers carrying what looked like a very healthy one-metre tall marijuana plant in a pot, while another was carrying a case of beer. I didn't want to hang around any longer so I turned the vehicle round, but just as we drove past our note-taker's house the police brought her out in handcuffs. She spotted us. As they led her away she shot us a look of absolute scorn.

I found out later that she had been charged with drug offences and with breaching laws pertaining to the alcohol management plan in force on Mornington Island. Things were not much better for our driver, who was said to be hungover after a night on the grog and was expected to be out of action for the rest of our stay. That was good news for us, since it meant that we could move about more freely and speak to whomever we wanted. In fact it became clear that a lot of people were scared of him and would not have spoken to us while he was around.

The day before we were due to leave the island I was contacted by a prominent community member, who asked if we could meet somewhere out of town as he didn't want to risk being seen talking to us. We followed his instructions and after picking him up we drove several kilometres to an area of bushland well hidden from the main road where we were confident we could not be seen.

As we sat in the car our informant began to make startling allegations of corruption within the Mornington Island Shire Council. After about half an hour we noticed an old blue sedan driving along another bush track which ran parallel to ours and was close enough for us to be able to see who was inside. As it approached, the driver slowed to a crawl—we immediately recognised our former chauffeur and note-taker, together with another male. They stopped, looked at us and then drove off.

I asked my informant if he was concerned that he had been seen in our company. 'Nah,' he said, 'I'll be OK.' He didn't sound very convincing.

To me, it felt like a brazen attempt to deter him and everyone else on the island from talking to us.

My colleague and I left the island feeling not just demoralised but traumatised by what we had witnessed. The conditions on Mornington Island contradicted in every way the reports we were used to hearing at the regular interdepartmental meetings we attended in Brisbane. According to these reports Mornington Island was a reasonably safe and well-run community. What we had seen was a violent, disease-ridden, dysfunctional place where children walked the streets at night because they were too frightened to sleep.

It absolutely beggared belief that my people could be living in such deplorable conditions: children raised in filth and squalor, in two-bedroom houses without working toilets or showers that were home to as many as twenty people and any number of mangy dogs. What made the situation even more unforgivable was that across the channel between Mornington Island and the mainland, just a short geographical distance away, were the Mt Isa mines and the Century Zinc mine at Lawn Hill, which contained some of Australia's most valuable mineral deposits.

When Murrandoo Yanner first told me how people lived on Mornington Island, I found it difficult to believe. Now I knew that those awful stories were true. If what we had witnessed on Mornington occurred in suburbs like Clayfield, Ascot, Hamilton, St Lucia and Windsor there would be a royal commission before you could blink an eye, but for remote Indigenous communities it was out of sight, out of mind.

During January and February 2005 I made two separate visits to Mornington Island. Many of the Indigenous inhabitants were afraid to talk to me but others were eager to speak up. Among the complaints and allegations I heard were: young girls between eight and fourteen years old were approaching contractors working on the island and offering sexual favours in return for alcohol and cigarettes; an extremely high incidence of parental neglect; ongoing problems with young people sniffing petrol and other solvents; repeated efforts to obtain funding for 'night patrols' and a safe house to protect mothers and children from domestic violence had been to no avail; Indigenous people were reluctant to go to the hospital because they were not treated with respect or dignity by some of the hospital staff.

Under the Beattie Government, Indigenous communities were assigned a so-called 'champion' who was either the director general or assistant director general of a state government department. Each champion was to take personal charge of an Indigenous community and to ensure that statutory services were being properly provided.

After returning to Brisbane I advised the director and the assistant director general of DATSIP that I intended to call a meeting which I wanted the government champion for Mornington Island, Ted Campbell, and his advisers to attend. At the meeting I described the atrocious scenes I had witnessed on the island. I also outlined allegations of corruption, nepotism, intimidation and the misappropriation of government funds. Ted Campbell and his staff confirmed that these accorded with previous reports they had received. He pointed out, however, that the Department of Local Government and Planning could only ask for information and had limited power to intervene as the Mornington Island council was autonomous under law.

Two months later I was still waiting for a response to the issues raised during the meeting. There had been no word from Ted Campbell, despite his promise to act on my report. In frustration I emailed Warren Hoey, the director general of DATSIP. I reminded him that I had given a personal undertaking to many people on Mornington Island to highlight their shocking plight and to make every effort to motivate government agencies to provide to the community of Mornington Island the services that other Queenslanders took for granted. I told Warren, 'I await any advice you may be able to provide to me so that I may in turn inform those people who have placed their faith and trust in me to try to initiate change for the better.'

I did not receive a response to my email or to my written report into the living conditions on Mornington Island, either from within my own department or from the government champion's office.

In late November 2010 I ran into a friend and former colleague who had accompanied me on numerous visits to Aboriginal communities throughout Cape York and the Gulf of Carpentaria. He told me he was working on Mornington Island and had been doing project work there for several months. When I asked him what conditions were like on the island, he told me that things had not improved—in fact they had got worse.

As I write this, in late 2015, I have no reason to believe that the situation has changed.

Epilogue

As a young uniformed constable, I was encouraged by my boss to apply for the detective training course at the police college in Chelmer. It was an exciting and challenging course that, if successfully completed, could lead to a sought-after posting at the Criminal Investigation Branch.

I was accepted and began the course in March 1974. Guest speakers gave lectures about all areas of policing: breaking and entering; homicide; fraud; auto theft; and vice. One of our lecturers was Detective Sergeant Jack Herbert of the Licensing Branch. Tall, well-groomed and immaculately dressed, he captivated the room as soon as he walked in. All of us looked up to him.

Herbert gave an impressive lecture, emphasising that if we wanted to join the CIB we would have to apply ourselves and diligently pursue our goal. Of all the qualities we would need to have, the one he stressed most was loyalty to the people we served with.

Before the end of the year I learnt that Jack Herbert had retired from the police force on medical grounds. The next time I heard Herbert's name mentioned was more than a decade later in the *Four Corners* report entitled 'The Moonlight State', which named Herbert as the bagman who collected bribes for corrupt police.

I often think back to that lecture he gave at the police college in 1974. Was Herbert sizing us up, wondering which of us he would one day be able to recruit into his network of crooked detectives? As the only Indigenous man in the room, I reckon I would have stuck out. One way or another, I usually have.